Guide to SEVILLE and her Province

PATRONATO PROVINCIAL
DE TURISMO DE SEVILLA

GUADALQVE

A mis amigos Pedro
y Lucre. con todo
mi cariño

[signature]

As this book was going to press
HRH P<small>RINCESS</small> E<small>LENA</small> <small>DE</small> B<small>ORBÓN</small>
<small>AND</small> D<small>ON</small> J<small>AIME</small> <small>DE</small> M<small>ARICHALAR</small>
were about to be married in Seville.

They chose this city for their great day and Seville,
elegant as ever, offered them all her history,
her monuments, her light and her aroma,
as well as the unconditional affection of her people,
because Seville always receives those who visit
her in such a special way that they are made to
feel more at home than when they are at home.

In this book we attempt to speak of the attractions
of Seville to help visitors get to know her,
but this is very difficult, if not impossible,
because there is no way to relate what it means
to feel Seville, you have to see her, live her in situ.

Come and let yourself fall in love with Seville.

We are waiting for you.

"Hospitality and generosity are distinctive traits of the Sevillian's personality"

KING JUAN CARLOS I

"Seville nourishes the cultural roots... that the Andalusian people have created as a plastic adornment for their religious feelings"

POPE JOHN PAUL II

"Fair is proud Seville, let her country boast her strength, bear wealth, her site of ancient days"

LORD BYRON

"The city aglow with flame would seem, as a flower, to have been condensed on the last petal..."

VICENTE ALEIXANDRE

"Oh, Sevilla! Allure, wit, lightness, grace and flattery, in her furthest past and still today. Sevillilla!"

RAFAEL ALBERTI

"Nights in Seville have a fragrance of their own"

CATHERINE DENEUVE

"A climate such as yours can only produce ardent people; I hope that light and success continue to play a part in the future of this wonderful land and in that of its people"

MIKHAIL GORBACHEV

"Una ciudad que acecha / largos ritmos, / y los enrosca / como laberintos. / Como tallos de parra / encendidos..."

FEDERICO GARCÍA LORCA

"Seville, that city so full of everything, light, smell... sensuality"

AVA GARDNER

"It is amazing how much Seville has changed in such a short time. Sevillians must be proud of their city"

JULIO IGLESIAS

"Blinded by her true beauty"

DUKE OF ALBA

"Seville, the city that has inspired the greatest lyric works written by the greatest composers"

PLÁCIDO DOMINGO

Contents

ALL ABOUT SEVILLE

All about Seville

In the first part of this book, *All about Seville,* we will be highlighting the extremely varied aspects of the city and its surroundings, as these are fundamental keys to knowing and understanding it better. We shall see that Seville is the result of the various cultures that have achieved a *sui generis* civilisation within the European context. In the brief historical analysis we include are to be found the facts and conditions that made this so; and we can decipher the result by looking at the city's architecture, handicrafts, and traditions. If we add to this the ecological wealth of the city's surroundings we will find that Seville is an ideal spot in which to transform everyday life into something extraordinary.

THE FLOWERS OF SEVILLE

Seville is characterised by the wide variety of flowering plants that adorn the city. In the streets, gardens, and patios of Seville, the flowers alternate throughout the year so that their fragrance and colour are eternal. Geraniums, jasmines, carnations, night jasmines, orange blossom, bougainvillaeas, oleanders...

THE TREES

In Seville's streets and avenues there are almost fifty species of trees and bushes which change in appearance with the seasons of the year. Orange trees, palms, and sycamores are the most common, but there are also hundred-year-old tulip trees, lemon trees, jacarandas, elms, maples, aspens, acacias... some of which flower even in summer, as in the case of the Jupiter's beard.

The *florist* is a traditional figure in Seville that reveals the Sevillian's love for flowers.

THE CLIMATE

Seville has an exceptional climate, with mean annual temperatures of 18.2^0. Summers are hot, the temperature averaging 25.6^0. The coldest month is January (10.7^0) and the hottest August (26.9^0). November is the wettest, with an average of 100 mm. The city enjoys 250 days of sunshine a year.

THE PARKS

The streets and avenues harbour numerous gardens. The range of origins of the plants and trees in these is remarkable. The city's main parks are María Luisa •_148_, El Alamillo and the Parque de los Príncipes. But there are also numerous peaceful gardens with a profusion of flowers, such as the Murillo •_85_, María Cristina •_124_ and Miguel de Mañara gardens •_128_.

The **common lizard** is traditional on the cool walls of Sevillian patios, specially on summer nights.

The **house martin**—*delichon urbica*—is 'the' bird of Seville, that most representative of the city. It resembles a lighter-coloured swift and flies around in thousands from late spring until the onset of winter. They flock together forming clamorous circles at dusk and, after spending the night gliding lethargically, recover their activity at dawn. They live in mud nests which they build under cornices and eaves, lining the interior with feathers and the cottony fruit of the nearby poplars.

You can see them in numerous places in the old part of the city: the Cathedral •_66_, Santa Marta, •_64_, Avenida de la Constitución •_125_, San Leandro •_112_, Cristo de Burgos •_113_, Alameda de Hércules •_105_... The most striking and well known colonies are at the Palacio de Yanduri in the Puerta de Jerez •_124_ and in the Casa de los Bucarelli in Calle Santa Clara •_102_. Along with the martins, thousands of swallows and swifts, hoopoes and goldfinches arrive around March from Africa. At night, owls may be heard.

THE GUADALQUIVIR AND THE SEA

Seville's river is the only navigable river in Spain and its links with the sea are absolute. The Guadalquivir rises in the Sierra de Cazorla mountains and is inhabited by trout and carp, spiny loaches, topminnows, yellow perch, blennies, eels, and three-spined stickleback. And gambusias, black bass… The last sturgeon roe caviar factory in Coria del Río closed in the 70's, although there are plans to reopen it. Nowadays, sailing towards the mouth of the river, you can find eeling and shrimping boats. Further on, near Doñana, the crayfish catchers work along the banks.

Trout

Carp

Yellow perch

An excursion sailing down to the mouth of the Guadalquivir is to be highly recommended. There are boating companies that provide such trips • *126*.

The Aquatic Ecology Station, in the Cartuja Island Technology Park (former Pavilion of Monaco), is primarily devoted to ichthyological research of the river Guadalquivir. Samples from the river are kept in a four hundred thousand litre aquarium and can be viewed from a transparent tunnel.

Two-banded bream   *Bass*

Ray

Just an hour from Seville, in Sanlúcar de Barrameda, you can find the famed seafood and the most exquisite fish: hake, moray, conger eels, ray, bream—including two-banded and striped bream—porgy, scad, bass, maigre, and sargo. Shrimp fishing is characteristic of Sanlúcar.

THE OLIVE GROVES

This is the traditional image of the Andalusian and Sevillian countryside. Cultivation of olives goes back to the times of al-Andalus and it is interesting to observe the different planting methods (haphazardly, in squares, in rectangles, and in quincunxes). A traditional figure in Andalusian social history is the *jornalero* who beats down the olives with a stick.

From the olives flows the most exquisite oil, once they have passed through the conical mill stones. The finest olives are pickled or put in brine and are essential at the table.

Thousands of acres of Seville's countryside are sown with sunflowers, which also yield oil. On this land there are also palmettoes and milk thistles.

In the olive groves live beetles and scorpions, feared for their sting, together with common rabbits and European tortoises. The skies are home to wood pigeons, starlings, night-owls, mouse-eating bats, barn-owls, vultures, and Pharaoh's chicken.

LAS MARISMAS

Doñana is the largest and most important natural park in Europe, designated world cultural heritage and a biosphere reserve, and is an area with an ecological wealth of the highest order. Between the Guadalquivir and the Atlantic, the park is comprised of immense fresh- and salt-water marshes, desert areas with gigantic dunes that are shifted by the *foreño* wind, and scrubland and areas of rockrose. It is inhabited by the imperial eagle and by Iberian lynxes and mongooses; by sultana birds, which only exist in Spain, flamingoes, grey herons, and otters; red and fallow deer, and wild boar. The area is rich in spurtgrass, bulrush, rockrose, rosemary, thyme, reed and rush; pine trees and cork oaks. In spring, camomiles cover the marsh waters.

Heron   *Flamingo*   *Wild board*

The Ecosystems

SIERRAS AND DEHESAS

Some of these are close to Seville • _162_ and _163_ and there you will find coniferous trees such as stone pines and larches and, in particular, Spanish firs. In riparian forests are to be found elms and chestnut trees, and, everywhere, cork oaks, holm oaks, gall oaks, strawberry trees, hawthorns, rosemary, wild olive trees, mastic trees, myrtles, and carob trees.

In Seville's sierras there are wolves, deer, and wild boar. They are also home to wildcats and badgers. In the clear streams there are otters and trout. In the skies, imperial and golden eagles, Bonelli's eagles, short-toed eagles, Pharaoh's chicken, griffon vultures, peregrine falcons…

Iberian pig and fighting bull raising and cork cropping are the traditional activities.

THE VINE

This is one of the traditional crops around Seville and produces wines of worldwide renown. The stock used and, above all, the climate, are the determining factors for its success. There are four main wine-growing areas, grouped together with their own _appellation d'origine:_ Jerez-Sanlúcar, Montilla-Moriles, the Condado de Huelva, and Seville's Aljarafe.

THE LAND AND ITS MINERALS

Albero is a golden yellow coloured soil which is famous throughout the world as it is highly valued for use in bullrings. It is common in the parks and gardens of Seville. The main quarries are in Alcalá de Guadaira.

The nearest mining areas are in Almadén de la Plata and El Real de la Jara, in the Sierra Norte • _162_. Nearby also are the deposits at Río Tinto, long associated with the English, where there is an interesting museum to visit. These are open-cast mines which yield copper, graphite, biotite, amethysts, feldspar, celestite, gypsum, rock salt, dolomite, malachite, chalcopyrite, barytes…

Puente romano en Sevilla

ROMAN SEVILLE

The present-day layout of Seville dates from the times of the Roman city of Hispalis, many remains still existing, such as the Roman aqueduct which brought water from Alcalá de Guadaira (Puerta de Carmona) and the columns of a former temple where the present day Calle Mármoles is to be found.

Italica, in the town of Santiponce close to Seville, retains streets, remains of houses, mosaics, drains… The amphitheatre, the third largest in the Roman empire, is perfectly conserved and its theatre was recently reconstructed.

The oldest architectural site in the region is to be found in the Tartessian remains at Tejada la Vieja and in the prehistoric Gandul dolmens at Alcalá de Guadaira. There are burial graves in Sanlúcar la Mayor and at Pithos in Carmona.

MOORISH AND MUDEJAR ARCHITECTURE

The development of Andalusian architecture from the arrival of the Moors and its progression through time may be appreciated in numerous remains such as these four spots in the Alcazar: the *Patio de las Muñecas*, the *Patio de las Doncellas* • _79_ (above), the courtroom, and the Hall of the Ambassadors • _78_.

The portals of the oldest temple in Seville, the church of Santa Ana in Triana, are also Mudejar, as are those of the churches of Santa Catalina *(above)* and San Isidoro.

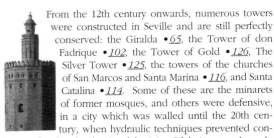

From the 12th century onwards, numerous towers were constructed in Seville and are still perfectly conserved: the Giralda • _65_, the Tower of don Fadrique • _102_, the Tower of Gold • _126_, The Silver Tower • _125_, the towers of the churches of San Marcos and Santa Marina • _116_, and Santa Catalina • _114_. Some of these are the minarets of former mosques, and others were defensive, in a city which was walled until the 20th century, when hydraulic techniques prevented continuous flooding by the Guadalquivir. Of their gates, the only ones remaining are the Postigo del Aceite • _129_ and those of Macarena and Cordova • _114_.

A traditional part of the artistic work of woodcraft is the coffered ceiling, which in Seville shows Mudejar influence, with its geometric tracery. This is visible today in many buildings. It combines the layout and the polychromy of wood, together with various other elements such as stone and stained glass.

Another example of vaults from al-Andalus times are the present-day churches of San Juan de la Palma, San Pedro, Santa Catalina, and Santa Marina.

The development of Gothic architecture in Seville may be observed by comparing the nave of Santa Marina (14th c.) *(above)* and that of the Cathedral (16th c.); or by comparing the portals of Santa Marina (14th c.), San Marcos (15th c.), and the Cathedral (16th c.).

GOTHIC ARCHITECTURE IN SEVILLE

The Gothic building par excellence in Seville is the Cathedral •_66_ *(above)*, the largest one in its style. The cathedral's ground plan is square and the five naves, of which the central one is the largest, are covered by 70 ogival vaults supported on 40 piers.

THE RENAISSANCE

Although there are many Renaissance buildings in the city, there are three which are particularly beautiful: the City Hall • _94_, with its pure Renaissance-style facade in the Plaza de San Francisco, the Archive of the Indies • _77_, with an interior patio and notable Doric columns, and the Andalusian Parliament, the former Hospital de las Cinco Llagas • _118_.

Archbishop's Palace

University

THE SEVILLIAN BAROQUE

Together with the Mudejar style, this is the foremost style in the city, the one which most attracts the visitor's attention. It is a local style, with numerous examples of outstanding architectural importance. The facades are exceptionally sumptuous: the Palacio de San Telmo • _142 (above)_, the Fine Arts Museum •_97_, the Archbishop's Palace • _64_, and the University • _144_.

Casa de Pilatos

Casa de Salinas

The Palaces

There are numerous buildings in the city that are the ultimate expression of Sevillian palatial architecture. These are luxurious buildings with gardens, stables, patios, and servants' dwellings. The Casa de Salinas, an ideal setting for gala dinners and receptions; the Palacio de los Marqueses de la Algaba (15th c.) • *119*, the Palacio de las Dueñas (15th c.) • *121*, the Palacio de Lebrija (15th c.) • *92*, the Casa de Pilatos (16th c.) • *110*, the Palacio de Monsalud (18th c.) • *100*.

Palacio de Lebrija

Palacio de los Marqueses de la Algaba

Palacio de las Dueñas

> *"Mi infancia son
> recuerdos de un
> patio de Sevilla,
> y un huerto claro
> donde madura el
> limonero..."*
>
> ANTONIO MACHADO

PATIOS

In Seville the patio is the fundamental element of typical dwellings, which is where family and social life has traditionally taken place. Noble patios of exquisite beauty are to be found in the following palaces: Yanduri and Guardiola • *124*, Dueñas • *121*, Mañara • *87*.

White and *albero* yellow are the local colours of Sevillian facades. The windows, oriels and balconies, the grilles and doors are characteristic.

In the first half of the 20th century Seville saw considerable growth of the school of so-called *regionalistic architecture*, the leading exponent of which was the great architect of the Iberoamerican Exposition of 1929, Aníbal González. There are interesting examples in many places, such as the Avenida de la Constitución • *125*.

However, an equally essential part of the city are the *patios* or *corrales de vecinos*, where residents base their lifestyle on familiarity and mutual support. Flowerpots of basil and mint are never absent among the geraniums, carnations, and night jasmines. It is in the Triana district where such patios find their greatest splendour.

In the streets there are numerous small altars and chapels, as in the accompanying picture, almost always of fine Sevillian pottery, along with bell gables and belfries of varying styles and periods.

A HOUSE IN THE COUNTRY

The most characteristic among Andalusian rural houses is the *cortijo,* with a particular structure which is still retained: chapel, *señorío* or landlord's quarters, granary, smithy, hay stores, coach house, stables, farmyards, patio, bedrooms, tenant's dwelling… An *hacienda olivarera* also has mills, a mill tower, and *tinahón* with buried earthenware storage tanks. There are a total of 260

haciendas catalogued, the closest being those of Guzmán (Seville), Los Ángeles (Alcalá de Guadaira), Torrequemada (Bollullos de la Mitación), La Buzona (Carmona), Loreto (Espartinas), El Rulo (Lebrija), Cortijo Águila Real (Guillena)…

The Universal Exposition held in Seville in 1992 left behind a number of buildings designed in accordance with the latest trends and equipped with the most advanced technology, unquestionably fine examples of contemporary Spanish architecture.

The Alamillo bridge, designed by the engineer Santiago Calatrava, is one of seven new bridges in Seville.

Santa Justa Railway Station (Antonio Cruz and Antonio Ortiz) is the first in the world specifically designed for the High-Speed Train and has received a number of prestigious architecture awards.

San Pablo International Airport was designed by the director of the Harvard School of Architecture, the Spaniard Rafael Moneo.

The Future Pavilion, by the architect Oriol Bohigas, and the Pavilion of Navigation, by Guillermo Vázquez Consuegra, are just two examples of the diversity of contemporary works on Cartuja Island.

The World Trade Centers Association manages the World Trade Center • *134*, the city's foremost *smart* building.

Arms of the Cathedral (Anon., 17th century)

PREHISTORY

The first settlements appear, leaving behind remains of dolmens and collective graves. The 'campanulate vessel' culture is established and commerce begins.

FIRST MILLENNIUM BC

The period of the great civilizations. Traces of the Tartessian kingdom. The Phoenicians introduce the practice of worshipping Hercules, patron of the city. Carthaginian colonization from 257 BC.

2ND CENTURY BC
5TH CENTURY AD

The Roman conquest. In 206 BC Scipio the African *(bust)* founds Italica. Hispalis arises shortly after. In 45 BC Julius Caesar makes it a Roman colony and calls it Julia Romula. The Roman emperors Trajan and Hadrian were born in Italica • *165*.

5TH CENTURY

Decline of Rome and invasion of the Vandals, who sack the city.

6TH CENTURY

Period of splendour under the Visigoths. Seville becomes a place of residence for monarchs and achieves religious unification. St. Leander and St. Isidore are two Sevillians with a place in History.

8TH CENTURY

This is the *al-Andalus* age. Abd ar-Rahman III gives the city the name of Ishbiliyah, and this is the beginning of a long period of religious tolerance. The Hispano-Roman aristocracy fuses with the invaders.

9TH AND 10TH CENTURIES

The city is under the rule of the Caliphate of Cordova, the most prosperous and cultured of the time.

11TH CENTURY

Seville becomes independent: the kingdom of Ishbiliyah is set up, whose greatest splendour is during the reign of al-Mutamid, the most beloved and remembered of the Moorish kings, even today. In the face of the Christian advance, the poet king seeks the aid of the Almoravids, who betray him and take power.

EL CARAMBOLO TREASURE

These are thought to be the jewels of Arganthonius, King of the Tartessians, who, it is related, established themselves on the banks of the Guadalquivir when their natural territory, Atlantis, disappeared under the waters.

The Phoenician navigator Melkart crossed the Straits of Gibraltar and, via the Guadalquivir, established Seville as a trade factory. Egyptians and Phoenicians considered him a hero, a saint and a god, and the Latins related him to Hercules, who was adopted by Seville as one of the city's patrons.

Seville's poet king, al-Mutamid, was be-

trayed and expelled from the city. His remains lie today in the Moroccan countryside, near Marrakesh. A Moorish chronicler relates: "The multitude crowded on the banks of the river; the women scratching their faces in grief".

How many cries, how many tears! What have we left now?

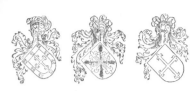

Christopher Columbus planned his voyage to the Americas in the Santa María de las Cuevas monastery •135, where his remains would later rest for several years

12TH CENTURY

The Almohad Age. King Abu Yaqub Yusuf constructs a new greater mosque, with its great minaret, the Giralda.

13TH CENTURY

Ferdinand III (the Saint) conquers Seville in 1248. The Castilian court is set up in the city, which is repopulated following the expulsion of the Moors. A considerable Jewish colony is established and the Mudejars (subjected Moors) arise. Alfonso X the Wise reigns in Seville and creates the General Literary Study.

14TH CENTURY

The time of Pedro I the Cruel, also called the Just. Seville's mosques are converted into Christian churches and the Alcazar is rebuilt. Decline of the prosperous Jewish community following the first great massacre of Jews in the country. Years of widespread epidemics.

15TH CENTURY

Completion of the Christian conquest. Seville is the seat of the Spanish Inquisition. The first printing press is set up. 1492 is the year America is discovered. A year later, Christopher Columbus enters Seville in triumph.

The Christian conquest of the city is reflected in its buildings. The mosques became churches and belfries and bell towers were added to their minarets, as in the case of the Giralda.

16TH CENTURY

Seville obtains the monopoly on trade with the Americas and the Casa de Contratación, or House of Trade, is set up. Seville is a hive of building activity with such important works as the Alameda de Hércules, the belfry section atop the Giralda and the Casa Lonja or Commodity Exchange. The city becomes the centre of Humanism with Antonio de Nebrija, Mateo Alemán and Hernando Colón. The Sevillian school of arts and letters is found, and the Corral de Comedias or Comedy Playhouse is established.

17TH CENTURY

Cervantes conceives *Don Quixote* whilst imprisoned in the Royal Gaol in Calle Sierpes. In 1610 the Moriscos are expelled and, seven years later, as a result of pressure by the city, the Papal Bull on the Immaculate Conception is issued. Floods and epidemics deplete the population considerably. The Indies fleet removes to Cadiz, thereby bringing about Seville's decline as a trade centre. Spain's first newspaper, the *Gaceta de Sevilla*, is established and the Comedy Playhouses are prohibited.

Social unrest during the 18th and 19th centuries led to the growth of banditry. One of the most famous bandits, Diego Corrientes, was executed in the Plaza de San Francisco in 1781.

18TH CENTURY

Work commences on the Tobacco Factory, the largest building in the country and seat of Seville's most important industry. Philip V sets up his Court in the city. In 1755 the city suffers the consequences of the Lisbon earthquake. Mayor Olavide designs the first scale map of Seville. Spain's first weekly is published and the General Archive of the Indies is founded.

OLAVIDE

"Hércules me fundó,
Julio César me cercó
de muros y torres altas,
y el rey santo me ganó..."

19th Century

During the Peninsular War against Napoleon, the Central *Junta* of the National Government is established in Seville (1810). The country's first steam vessel is built at the city's shipyards, and social unrest leads to the growth of banditry. The School of Bullfighting is created in the San Bernardo district. Gustavo Adolfo Bécquer writes his *Rimas y Leyendas*. Isabella II finances some important works: the Triana bridge and the Plaza Nueva. The April Fair is held for the first time. The Duke and Duchess of Montpensier set up their 'little Court' in Seville, at the Palacio de San Telmo, currently the seat of the Andalusian regional government. During the First Republic, Seville proclaims itself an independent canton and a Federal Constitution for Andalusia is planned. The newspaper *El Correo de Andalucía*, now Seville's oldest daily, is founded in 1898.

Los duques de Montpensier

**"Andaluces levantaos /
pedid tierra y
libertad. /
Sean por
Andalucía libre, /
España y la
Humanidad"**

20th Century

Profound economic backwardness causes serious social conflict, giving rise to the birth of Andalusian anarchism. In 1915 the notary public Blas Infante creates the Andalusian Centre and the Liberalist *Juntas* of Andalusia. Four years later, the Andalusian motto, arms and flag are adopted. Caciquism and the oligarchy continue to be the essential features of the structure of society, with considerable opposition from the intellectuals. Antonio Machado is born in Seville. This is the city of the 1927 generation of poets: Vicente Aleixandre, Luis Cernuda, Federico García Lorca, Rafael Alberti, who come to Seville at the invitation of the bullfighter Ignacio Sánchez Mejías.

Alfonso XIII gives his backing to the Iberoamerican Exposition of 1929 and to the transformation of the city undertaken by regionalistic architects. Following the Second Republic, Seville is the first Spanish city to be taken after General Franco's uprising. The Building Ordinance allows the plundering of the city's architectural heritage for the next 30 years.

In 1980, Seville sees the largest demonstration in its history calling for regional autonomy. In 1982, the Andalusian people elect their first regional parliament. A few months later, two politicians from Seville, Felipe González and Alfonso Guerra, leaders of the PSOE, the Spanish socialist party, form Spain's longest-lasting democratic government. In 1992 Sevilla hosts the Universal Exposition.

Blas Infante, father of Andalusian nationalism

Sevillian Felipe González, undisputed leader of Spanish socialism, has been the country's Prime Minister since 1982.

In 1992 Seville hosted the Universal Exposition, which, under the theme of the Age of Discovery, achieves record participation and attendance.

Work is also done on floats and platforms for the Holy Week processions, for which cedar, white pine, Guatemala cedar, and mahogany is used. A traditional part of the artistic work of woodcraft is the coffered ceiling. It was the Mudejar influence, with its geometric tracery, which gave rise to its final form.

The manufacture of horse-drawn carriages is a centuries-old tradition. Workshops in Seville, Carmona, Alcalá de Guadaira, and Dos Hermanas today restore carriages such as light barouches, phaetons, spider phaetons, charres, broughams, galeras, dogcarts, peters, landaus, calashes, char-a-bancs, berlins, sociables, omnibuses and *chavalas*. In this work, they use oak wood, holm oak, poplar, and acacia.

HANDICRAFTS

Seville is a distinctive and unique centre for Spanish and Andalusian crafts. This is so because of the complexity of its history and the abundance and diversity of the social groups that have distinguished the city for centuries. The assimilation of the culture of the first civilisations, and the influence provided by Rome, Islam, Christian Spain, and the Italian Renaissance, gave rise to the adoption of innumerable handicrafts with particular differentiating features. Features which may be explained by the Sevillian's way of life and by his special feeling for the city's feast days, traditions, and religious feelings.

The inhabitants of the city impart to their Holy Week a fervour that is linked to scenographical representation of images. It is here, in the vitality of the representation and its surroundings, where the need for the work of numerous craft workers directly linked to what is traditional in Seville • *49* arises. But, at the same time, there are other activities which bear the mark of tradition, such as the pottery and tile-making which survive in Triana, and the saddler and harnesser's craft which are still to be found around the populous Arenal • *128*.

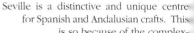

THE ART OF WOODCRAFT AND ITS CRAFTSMEN

Both civil and religious cabinetmaking still have genuine craftsmen in Seville and Carmona. Classical mahogany furniture and limoncillo marquetry, console tables, and cornucopia mirrors. Traditional Sevillian furniture has always been polychromatic, with a base of a main colour, usually green or red, to which is applied a detailed decoration of flowers and other similar items. And this is applied to rush-bottomed chairs, tables, headboards, coffers, trunks, chests of drawers…

Seville is the main centre in Spain for traditional image-making. Juan Martínez Montañés *(left)* was the founder of the Seville school • *48*.

METALWORK

As a result of the great growth seen by Seville in business, civil, and religious affairs from the 15th century on, iron forging became one of the most outstanding crafts. Names such as Fray Francisco de Salamanca, Hernando de Pineda, and Francisco Ocampo are just a few examples from a long list of blacksmiths who have done noteworthy work in Seville. Artistic ironworking continues to prosper at a number of forges in Seville, Carmona, and Puebla

de Cazalla, where the forge is still used to heat the iron, the anvil to work it, hammers, tongs, punches, files, chisels, cold sets… Instruments which are used for stretching, widening, sharpening, relieving, and jumping-up. In this way are made grilles, doors, iron gates, balconies, lamps, lanterns, oil lamps, and andirons.

LEATHER

One of the handicrafts for which Andalusia and Seville have always stood out is saddlery. A *vaquero*-style saddle has a cowhide pommel and a pig leather rear support, and the saddler finishes the seat off with sheepskin.

Saddlery instruments: awls, needles, piercing tools, cotter pins, semicircular gouges, and chisels, the tool which best symbolises the saddler's craft and which is used as a knife.

In addition to saddles, English, Hungarian, and calash harnesses are made, with their tassels and bells. And harnesses for popular carriages such as *manolas*, light barouches, and hackneys.

For chaps and riding boots, cowhide is used, and for the adornments cat and gazelle skin.

GOLD AND SILVERSMITHS

The history of Sevillian gold and silversmiths dates back to ancient times and persists in present-day workshops which are linked to religious works for Holy Week. *(Above: the float of the Cristo de la Pasión • 92).*

The Alphonsine Tables, the leading work of Spanish medieval orfevrerie, include decorations upon

a chiselled background comprising enamel, an abundance of emeralds and amethysts, agate cameos, heraldic motifs, religious images, in addition to one or two less usual iconographic items such as the female with a unicorn • 74. On the left, the windowed case with the body of Saint Ferdinand • 68.

Tartessian jewels, such as the Carambolo treasure, • 23 and 150, display a characteristic uniform style.

Juan Herrera, with works in the Victoria & Albert Museum in London; Francisco de Alfaro, author of the Cathedral tabernacle; and Juan Laureano de Pina, who worked the silver case with the body of Saint Ferdinand • 68, are examples of famous gold and silversmiths from Seville.

The Discovery of America had positive, determining repercussions for Sevillian orfevrerie. The gold and silver from the New World found in Seville's workshops masterful hands that worked universal jewels.

The tradition has lasted up to the present in all its purity. The transmission of gold and silver-working down the centuries gave rise to a group of craftsmen of the highest quality and virtually unique in Spain (Marmolejo, Villarreal, Seco Velasco).

Pottery was the most brilliant expression of the Tartessian civilisation, where the phenomenon of the campanulate vessel is an outstanding example.

The Italian *Niculoso Pisano* incorporated wall tile techniques in the 16th century.

POTTERY

The oldest painted pottery in western Europe is on exhibit in the Seville Archaeological Museum • *150*. This is from the Tartessian culture and was found a few kilometres from Seville at the Carambolo site. From that time on, a long pottery tradition has impregnated the city. Roman and Moorish techniques came together with Renaissance cus-

toms brought over by *Niculoso Pisano*, the great Italian craftsman who introduced wall tile techniques to Seville in the 16th century. Pisano has two famous altarpieces in the Alcazar • *79* and he is also the author of the pottery portal of the church of Santa Paula • *115*.

The palace of the Marquis of Tarifa, known by the name of Casa de Pilatos • *110*, deserves consideration as a genuine Sevillian wall tile museum.

Sevillian pottery is still made in the traditional workshops in the Triana neighbourhood • *132*, where the Santa Ana, Altozaño, and Montalbán factories enjoy a high reputation.

The pottery manufactured by the English Pickman family in the former Cartuja Monastery • *135* is still made a few kilometres from Seville.

The nearby town of Lebrija has traditionally stood out for its manufacture of consumer pottery. The modelling and drying in the shade of earthenware jars, pitchers, and flowerpots is a characteristic feature of the town.

Pottery was traditionally made on the potter's wheel and using a log kiln. Nowadays, tools for turning and moulding, as well as ovens and electric wheels are used.

Venery pottery has been one of the main contributions of Sevillian pottery.

The *Andalusíes* showed themselves to be great and refined gastronomists. They abolished the custom of eating in the kitchen and promoted 'dining rooms'. The ritual began and ended with the washing of hands. It was the Omeya dynasty that established an order for serving the dishes, as formerly they were all served at once. First of all, the broths and soups were brought to the table; secondly, the cold hors d'oeuvres, pickled fish, stewed and roast meat, and, finally, the sweets.

Because of its geographical situation and historical circumstances, Seville has been the channel for numerous exchanges in eating habits, both between the East and the West and between Europe and the Americas. At this crossroads, the spices brought by the Moors converged with the traditional Mediterranean olive and vine culture, which in turn crossed the Atlantic and received hitherto unknown products and condiments. The first potatoes, tomatoes and corn to arrive from the New World were planted in Calle Sierpes.

Paprika, of which *La Pitorra* is the most popular, is one of the spices of Arabic origin that are fundamental in Andalusian cuisine. Others are pepper, cinnamon, coriander, and cumin.

ANISETTE
Cazalla and Constantina are the centres of a wine-growing district which has been transformed into a liquor-producing one. The aguardientes produced in this area are known by the generic name of *cazalla*. This is a beverage which is famed for being hard and strong. Various types of aniseed-based liquors are made: sweet, dry, semi-sweet, and a range of coffee, mint, orange, etc. liqueurs and creams.

WINES

Andalusia offers some of the wines with most personality in the world. The generous Jerez-Xéres-Sherry wines, together with those from Montilla-Moriles, Condado de Huelva, and Seville's Aljarafe, have no rivals. They are the happy

result of climate and soil conditions that are unique in the world and the expertise of the men involved. Wines called *generous*, elaborated in *botas*—oak barrels. The most popular are *fino*, biologically grown; *mosto* or must, which is consumed in the early stages of fermentation; and *solera*, wine in the last stage of fermentation, i.e. the wine which remains in the lower row of barrels on the floor • *166*.

OLIVE OIL

Andalusia is fortunate enough to possess the most extensive and traditional olive groves. This means that culinary habits are particularly marked by the use of olive oil. For Sevillian cuisine, olive oil is not a fat that is necessary for cooking, but an essential condiment for its dishes. The best olive oil is *virgin*, obtained from the first cold pressing of the olives. It is usually greenish or golden yellow, and its flavour is the fruitiest. The following pressings produce an olive oil of a more neutral flavour and of a paler colour.

Cured ham, which is aromatic and of the finest meat, is the best accompaniment to a good fino wine. It is a matchless product which comes from Iberian pigs which have been fed exclusively on acorns. The unique microclimate which exists in its region of origin (Sierra de Aracena and Sierra Norte) makes it the most famous ham in the world. It is popularly known as *pata negra*, black leg, because of its dark hoof.

Seville olives form an essential part of any dining table in Andalusia. There are 'fat' olives, pickled olives, olives prepared in brine, stuffed with anchovies or sweet peppers or almonds...

The fresh **seafood,** from the Atlantic Ocean near the mouth of the Guadalquivir, that is consumed in Seville is of exceptional quality. There are no finer shrimps than those from Sanlúcar, nor more exquisite wedge shells than those from Ayamonte or Isla Cristina. All manner of prawns and shrimps, and spring murices are among the finest seafoods from our coast which, of course, also contributes the best fish: sole, plaice, gilthead, dentex, mullet, anchovies.

Seville is a very special orange grove. The bitter oranges that adorn the city's avenues and squares each year supply a considerable part of the English marmalade industry.

CONVENT SWEETS

Ora et labora becomes deliciously real in the sweets made by the nuns in Seville's convents. With a prominent position in Sevillian confectionery, the range of products offered by the majority of Seville province's 40 convents is extremely varied. You cross the convent atrium, or *compás,* and come to the revolving window, where you announce your presence with the bell. A soft voice will cry *¡Ave María Purísima!,* to which you reply *¡Sin pecado concebida!* and place your order. You put the money on the turntable, turn it and the home-made sweet, a divine temptation, will then appear: *yemas* from the convent of San Leandro in Seville • *112* (the recipe for which only the Archbishop of Seville is entitled to know), or from the St. Clare nuns at Alcalá de Guadaira. 'Moroccan' cakes from Écija, marzipan from the Estepa enclosure... and, returning to Seville, Santa Inés buns • *113* (a medieval pastry made of bread, oil, sesame, and sugar), or Santa Paula quince jelly and jam • *115*. All of these may be acquired at a small establishment in the Pasaje de los Seises • *77*, opposite the cathedral.

All about Seville

Tapas

Tapas, or snacks, and the custom of going out for tapas are a long-standing Sevillian tradition. Seville's bars provide customers with a traditional list of tapas, which are usually recited orally by the waiter as he serves the beer or wine ordered on arrival. The bar and street terraces are the places preferred by Sevillians to enjoy these small, extremely varied dishes. Apart from seafood, cured meats, preserves, and salted dishes, Sevillian bars prepare cooked tapas, a veritable recipe book of the genuine Sevillian cuisine. Some such places are: El Costalero

(left), Casa Morales, and El Rinconcillo *(below)* • *114*.

In any popular bar or restaurant you can try cooked or fried vegetables: stuffed artichokes, spinach Seville style, wild asparagus, fried green peppers. In addition to these, snails, oxtail, *pringá* (a mixture of the meat, black pudding, and bacon fat resulting from a *cocido* or stew), tripe, Flemish eggs, various types of *pavía* (battered fish), or dogfish in yellow sauce are also very common tapas, not to mention, of course, a long list of *aliños* dressed with genius and extravagance.

Pescaíto Frito

The fish shop is an establishment that forms an essential part of Seville's social fabric and is closely linked to family suppers. It is normal to buy paper cones of fried fish for supper at home (between eight and ten at night) or, better still, eat them on the terrace of some nearby bar. It is the special way of frying used by these establishments that gives them their universal fame • 129.

The fish shop's wares are always on view, and are sold by weight. For four hungry people a good supper is a quarter kilo of hake, a quarter of squid (which is usually cuttlefish, masterfully prepared), a quarter of marinated dogfish, a quarter of fried roe, a quarter of fried shrimps, and, finally, a quarter of croquettes, especially when there are children. You can also buy from the fish shop the accessories for such a tasty dish: radishes, capers, a few olives. And, of course, regañá, a kind of flat, hard bread that is ideal for accompanying the fried fish.

Breakfast in Seville is another genuine feature that has no equal. In virtually any bar in the city you may have breakfast at particularly reasonable prices. It is a widespread custom to have breakfast away from home and this has given rise to a broad range of options, almost always based on white coffee and the traditional toasted bread. The toast in question may be made from serrano bread, *viena, bollo,* or *mollete.* It may be spread with butter, lard, olive oil with or without garlic, various types of paté, ham… Above, the classic Bar Laredo • 93.

A typical breakfast in Andalusia is *churros,* also known as *calentitos.* Like the fish shops, *churrerías* are typical establishments which are only open at certain hours (in this case, from about 8 to 11). It is interesting to watch how the long 'wheels' of churros are fried, the skill of the *churrero* with the sticks he uses to separate them and that of his wife, who handles them just out of the boiling oil. They are also fried in small rings, called *papas* because they were formerly made with potatoes, although now with the same ingredients: flour and water. It is customary to allow people to eat their churros in a nearby bar provided they order at least a coffee. They are bought by weight and there is always a price list on view. Best of all is the *porra,* the hub of the wheel. There is a *churrería* in Calle Arfe, near the Postigo del Aceite.

RECIPE FOR GAZPACHO

Gazpacho is the traditional food of the Andalusian countryside. The labourers used to take advantage of the oil from the olive groves to have a nutritious and refreshing lunch. It is a cold soup made from olive oil, bread, garlic, tomato and peppers.

There are varying types of gazpacho, depending on the region within Andalusia, the village, and the family. *Salmorejo* is a very thick gazpacho, served with ham and hard-boiled egg. *Ajoblanco* replaces the tomato with almonds. It is a product that is prepared daily in summer in most Sevillian homes and something that is usually offered to visitors as a mark of hospitality. It is, of course, also served in restaurants and bars. It may be eaten with a dressing as a first course or simply in a glass to accompany the meal. It can also be a dessert or be drunk at any time to calm one's thirst and the heat.

"A clove of garlic per person, salt to taste, and oil as you wish"

Ingredients for 4 people: 3 ripe tomatoes; 2 small cloves of garlic; a green, not too hot, pepper; half a cucumber; 100 grams of the previous days' bread; one or two tablespoons of vinegar; five or six tablespoons of virgin olive oil; one teaspoon of cooking salt; half a glass of water.

1 Cut all the vegetables into small pieces. Soak the bread. Peel the cucumber and garlic, and remove the stalks and seeds from the peppers.

2 Place all the ingredients in the electric mixer, in this order: first, the garlic and the cucumber, followed by the peppers, tomatoes, bread, salt, vinegar and oil.

3 When you obtain the desired consistency, a light cream, add water, salt, oil, and vinegar to suit your particular taste.

4 Sieve the mixture with a wide-gauge sieve.

5 Serve chilled accompanied by a dressing if wished.

Dressings in Seville usually consist of onion, cucumber, peppers, tomato, bread, ham, or hard-boiled egg, all finely chopped.

DRESSINGS ARE SERVED FINELY CHOPPED ON A TRAY SO THAT EACH PERSON MAY HELP HIMSELF AS DESIRED.

Musical composition in Seville, as with most of the arts, has always been influenced by the diversity of different cultures that have existed in the city. Along with the first flamenco *tonás,* an art that was hidden until the 19th century, musical scores have survived from the long Islamic period. But it was above all in the busy years at the time of the Discovery of America when the *cultured* music composed in Seville reached a position of international importance which still persists. Today one can acquire, in any establishment, the music of the great composers of that age, such as Cristóbal de Morales or Francisco Guerrero, masterfully and faithfully interpreted by the Taller Ziryab.

Abd ar-Rahman II commissioned Ziryab, the famous musician, to disseminate the novelties of Eastern music throughout the lands of his Caliphate. His teachings gave rise to numerous Arabic-Andalusian melodies, in addition to contributing to the modification of the native dances and tunes of the region.

Joaquín Turina *(left)* is Seville's great composer. Internationally famous, he turned his sights to Andalusia to compete in Paris with the Russian themes by Stravinsky that achieved fame at the beginning of the century. In this way, Turina gained popularity with works such as *Danzas Gitanas, Danzas Fantásticas,* and the *Seville Suite.*

Opera is a traditional genre in Seville, much respected inasmuch as the city has been the inspiration for some of the most famous works. *Carmen* and *The Marriage of Figaro* have gained numerous opera fans in Seville, which since 1992 has one of the world's best opera houses • *127.*

"Près des remparts de Séville / Chez mon ami Lillas Pastia / j'irai danser la séguedille et boire du manzanilla"
(CARMEN)

"Siviglia, Leonora, oggi Siviglia é a casa mía"
(DON GIOVANNI)

Gaditan Manuel de Falla, one of the great musicians of the 20th century (shown here on a 100 Pta note), left his greatest love in Seville: the *Bética* Orchestra, today the city's Philharmonic orchestra. His *Amor Brujo* and the *Retablo de Maese Pedro* are known throughout the world.

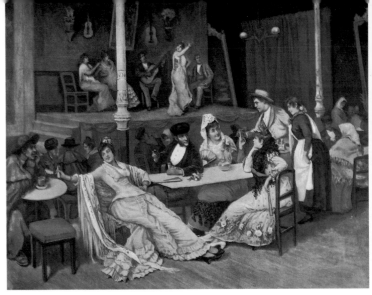

FLAMENCO MUSIC

A particularly popular style of music, flamenco has its roots in the *toná*, the most primitive form of song, which arose from Byzantine liturgical music which the Church adopted in Spain in the 11th century. It was strongly influenced by centuries of Moorish culture—which impregnated it with feeling—and, above all, by the persecution of the *Moriscos* (baptised Moors) and gypsies decreed by the Catholic Monarchs. Flamenco began to become timidly known from the 18th century, when, during the reign of Charles III, the capture of *Moriscos* was outlawed. It has been during the past century when flamenco has abandoned its intimacy and has become a public entertainment. Today

it is considered the *soul* of all that is Andalusian, especially in Seville, which is the geographical centre of the history of flamenco.

The Spanish pavilion at the 1900 Universal Exposition in Paris gave a flamenco performance which was attended daily by the great all-time composer, Claude Débussy *(left)*. According to Federico García Lorca "he, who had his soul open to the four winds of the spirit, was impregnated by our old music, our old complaints, and by our old and new rebelliousness."

"The Inquisition, the persecution and flight, the blood, violence, fear and superstition, wailing and joy, rebelliousness and oppression, are the roots of this art."

"Silverio Franconetti, the great revolutionary, the ancestral and thousand year old bird that, with amazing effort, extracted to the curb of the well the water stored for centuries in its depths by the springs of the people."

The various song forms. From the old *toná* comes the *martinete*—just the singer's voice and the sound of the forge hammer, and the *siguiriya,* as tragic as it is beautiful. From the latter arises the *serrana,* through the *livianas.* The *soleares* have significance in themselves though they came about as an accompaniment to dancing. Related to these are the *polo, bulerías,* and *alboreas.* And, influenced by them are the *cantiñas, alegrías, romeras, mirabrás, caracoles…* Another *palo* of flamenco is to be found in the *tango,* from which the *tientos* developed. Variants are *fandangos, sevillanas, villancicos,* and the *garrotín.*

With the death of *Camarón de la Isla,* flamenco music has lost one of its greatest performers. Other famous flamenco artists were the Niña de los Peines, Tía Anica la Piriñaca, Joaquín el de la Paula, Manolito María, Pepe Marchena, Juan Breva, Manolo Caracol and Antonio Mairena. But we can still listen live to Fernanda and Bernarda de Utrera, José Meneses, Enrique Morente, Curro Malena, El Lebrijano, Naranjito de Triana, Paquera de Jerez, Chocolate, Juan Varea, Juanito Valderrama, El Cabrero, Fosforito, Manuel Mairena, José el de la Tomasa, Calixto Sánchez…

Camarón de la Isla

Fernanda and Bernarda   *Naranjito de Triana*   *Antonio Mairena*   *La Niña de los Peines*

A seductive dance for the woman to show herself off, present-day **sevillanas** are divided into four sections. It is an elegant and sensuous dance which Sevillians learn from their childhood years. Any celebration is an excuse to organise a good time with sevillanas. Whether well or badly, everyone in Seville sings and dances sevillanas. There are many composers and each year, during the April Fair, new sevillanas are presented to the public.

Bulerías join their thirds dragged along by the vertiginous rhythm of the guitar and the dancing.

Flamenco clubs are formed by fans and are common to the neighbourhoods and villages of Seville. At weekends, they organise song and dance performances, and, in Spring and Summer, numerous festivals in which one may appreciate the real vitality of flamenco. These festivals are attended by the best flamenco singers and guitarists. The various events are publicised in the local press, usually on Fridays.

El Pali   *Romero San Juan*

Seville is still mourning the death of Paco Palacios *El Pali,* a popular sevillana composer. *Romero San Juan* has created one of the most beautiful sevillanas: *"Pasa la vida igual que pasa la corriente / cuando el río busca al mar / y yo camino indiferente / donde me quieran llevar."*

Guitars and Castanets

A musical instrument found throughout the world, the guitar is directly derived from the Moorish zyrab or quitâra, which was used in Seville for centuries to accompany the Arabic-Andalusian melodies. In the 19th century, the maestro Antonio Torres created the present-day guitar with six strings and from this renewal arose the main guitar-making schools.

Guitars are made entirely by hand, although some luthiers use small machines for rounding and smoothing.

La Guitarra

*Empieza el llanto
de la guitarra.
Se rompen las
copas
de la madrugada.
Empieza el llanto
de la guitarra.
Es inútil
callarla. Llora
monótona como
llora el viento
sobre la nevada.
Es imposible
callarla.
Llora por cosas
lejanas.
Arena del Sur
caliente
que pide camelias
blancas.
Llora flecha sin
blanco,
la tarde sin
mañana,
y el primer pájaro
muerto
sobre la rama.
¡Oh guitarra!
Corazón malherido
por cinco espadas.*

**Federico
García Lorca**

Luthiers need to master various craft activities, such as cabinet-making, varnishing and marquetry. In Seville, Francisco Barba *(right)* makes guitars to order, from cedar, fir and cypress wood (Calle Arroyo 20). There are other workshops at Calle Covadonga 9 and Calle Pozo 20.

Paco de Lucía, universal artist, whose guitar best expresses the depth of flamenco music.

The castanet is a fundamental percussion instrument which marks the rhythm in flamenco dancing. Castanets are held between the fingers and made to sound whilst dancing. The only craft workshop which makes them from cherry wood is at Calle Bordadores 3-5C.

FLAMENCO DRESS AND ACCESSORIES

The frilled gypsy or flamenco dress is a common garment for Sevillian women and is only used at fairs and pilgrimages. It has its origins in the primitive fairs of the 18th century. There are various types, depending on the use to be given. Its main characteristic is its immense flare and the frills, which bring out a woman's beauty. The best dresses are those made of satin, poplin, and organdie, and nowadays there is a return to the styles used in mid century: an abundance of cotton frills, tassels, bone lace, and embroidered silk shawls.

Embroidery and needlework have always been traditional handicrafts in Seville. Silk embroidery had its own quarter in the city and there are numerous famous schools whose work is on show in various museums. Embroidered shawls are white for going to bullfights and black for Easter Thursday. The *mantón de Manila,* an embroidered silk shawl, is also a garment which characterises Seville women and is used on any festive occasion. Nowadays they are made by craft workshops at Calle García de Vinuesa 33 and Argote de Molina 18.

In the country, at fairs and on pilgrimages, men use a *traje corto,* short suit, which is ideal for horse-riding.

And, as protection from the Sun, a wide-brimmed hat known as *sombrero cordobés.*

The *peina* or *peineta* is an essential accessory when a woman dresses up, whether for a gypsy dress or to accompany a shawl. They are made of celluloid and tortoiseshell and the craftsman uses nothing more than a marquetry saw. In Seville there is only one workshop that makes them; it was founded in 1936 and is at Calle Don Pedro Niño 17.

The high temperatures in Seville have turned the fan into a popular item. There are painted fans, lace fans, folding fans…

"Cuando se lanza contra el enemigo, los luceros se cansan de seguirlo y las nubes le pierden el rastro."

BEN ABU-L-HAYTAM,
Moorish-Andalusian poet

The **Andalusian horse**, of Arabian descent, is much appreciated as a saddle horse. It is somewhat smaller than an English thoroughbred, shorter in the neck and body, with rounder hindquarters, a higher tail and a dapple-grey coat. It is not a fast horse, nor one for resistance, but its movements are noble and majestic. Of medium height, the Andalusian horse crossed the Atlantic at the time of the Discovery of America and the majority of present-day breeds in the Americas are descended from it, for example the *criolla*. Nowadays there are Andalusian horses of various lineages: the *Guzmans, Valenzuelas, cartujanos, romanitos, Terrys...*

*"En un caballo andaluz
De la generosa raza
Que al sacro Guadalquivir
Le suele pastar la grama:
Castaño oscuro, fogoso,
Cabos negros, gruesas ancas,
Ancho pecho, recios brazos,
Corto cuello, cola larga,
Chica cabeza y orejas,
Crines grandes, encrespadas,
Gallardo, brioso y fiero..."*

CELÍN DE ESCARICHE

*"Otro nuevo Alejandro
en vos conoce
El caballo andaluz,
que a vuestra mano
la boca rinde, y toma el
duro freno."*

BALTASAR DE ESCOBAR

*"La corrida del domingo
no se encierra sin mi jaca.
Mi jaca la marismeña,
que por piernas tiene alas.*

*Venta vieja de Eritaña
la cola de mi caballo
dos toros negros
peinaban..."*

FERNANDO VILLALÓN

Fighting bulls are carefully selected and bred so as to give their best in the bullring in nobleness, breed and bravery. The most reputed stock farms are situated in the triangle formed by Jerez, Seville, and Cordova. A one-year-old bull is called *añojo*, a two-year-old a *becerro*. When three, it is called a *utrero*, and a *novillo* is a four year old bull.

Miura

Bohórquez

Domecq

Jandilla

Pablo Romero

The most important stock farms are: Miura, Guardiola, Pablo Romero, Bohórquez, Núñez, Domecq, Buendía, Jandilla, Rojas, Manolo González, Ordoñez, Peralta, Puerta…

The *garrochista* or herdsman armed with a goad is a common sight on Andalusian farms where fighting bulls are raised. It is also a sporting activity.

Lagartijo

Joselito el Gallo and Juan Belmonte

Curro Romero

The greatest bullfighters of all time have been traditionally linked to Seville and its fans. Bombita, Frascuelo, Lagartijo, Chicuelo, Guerrita, Gitanillo de Triana, Manolete, Joselito el Gallo and Juan Belmonte are outstanding figures in Sevillian bullfighting, as are Curro Romero, Espartaco, Emilio Muñoz, etc. today.

The origins of bullfighting date back to the 16th and 17th centuries, when it was practised by the nobility and received the full backing of the House of Austria. Philip V, the first Bourbon king, was educated at Versailles and was also the first anti-bullfighting monarch. But his successor Ferdinand VII was the promoter of the School of Bullfighting and Alfonso XIII was chairman of the *Maestranza de Caballería*.

Sevilla.   *Salida de los toros.*

The Baratillo arena has belonged to an ancient Order linked to Spanish royalty since the 18th century, the *Maestranza de Caballería*. Towards the end of the 18th century, this famous bullring was redesigned and took on its present appearance. Nowadays every bullfighter's greatest dream is to be taken out of the ring on the shoulders of his fans through the Puerta del Príncipe *(left, Curro Romero).* The bullfighting season commences on Easter Sunday and continues until around Michaelmas, in autumn. The leading bullfighters perform at this arena every year, particularly during the April Fair. A visit to the Real Maestranza is to come close to the very heart of bullfighting •*127*.

1. The wait, the suit, prayers, the parade.

3. The **kill**. In this ultimate instant, the bullfighter prepares for the final *estocada* or thrust.

2. The three **stages.** The first stage is the *varas* or goad stage, to ascertain the bull's condition. Next, the *banderillas* stage, to check its state after the initial punishment. In the *muletas* or cape stage, the bullfighter and the bull are alone in the ring, face to face.

4. The **rewards**. The grandstands in Seville are occupied by aficionados who are discerning, tolerant and, in a way, cruel. The public is the ultimate judge. *Silence*, which may be 'heard' in a very special way at the Maestranza, is a symbol of expectancy or a punishment. And there is a scale of rewards: applause, lap of honour, ears and tail, or—the highest honour— leaving the ring through the Puerta del Príncipe.

HOMBRERAS
CORBATÍN
ALAMARES
CHAQUETILLA
MEDIAS

CASTAÑETA O COLETA
CHALECO
FAJÍN
CAPOTE DE PASEO

MONTERA
CAPOTE
TALEGUILLA
MACHOS
ZAPATILLAS

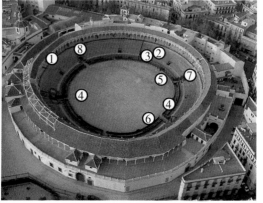

1. **BOXES**

2. **GRANDSTANDS**

3. **BARRIERS**

4. **PASSAGE**

5. **REFUGES**

6. **CUADRILLA ENTRANCE**

7. **BULLPEN GATE**

8. **BULL EXIT**

The April Fair is Seville's foremost festivity. A city made of canvas and Chinese lanterns rises on the outskirts, offering Sevillians fun and merriment for an entire week. The atmosphere is marked by horseback riding during the day and the activity in the *casetas* at night. *Sevillanas* dancing, singing, and a glass of wine are the keys, and the social gatherings among friends and family are the symbols. The women come in their *flamenco* dresses even when not riding horseback. Even if one does not have acquaintances with private *casetas*, the Fair offers the outsider no end of *casetas* that open their doors to all.

The fairground is an ephemeral city. Its streets are planned and signposted with the names of famous bullfighters, and the *casetas* are numbered as in any street anywhere in the world.

The **horse promenade** during the day is one of the most beautiful sights that can be seen. Thousands of horses are brought to the Fair to be ridden by elegant horsemen and lady riders; this sight is a special attraction at the fairground. Hundreds of barouches, landaus, phaetons, and calashes are also on parade.

Families, groups of friends or professionals, associations, and institutions have a **caseta** at the Fair so that members can sing, dance, eat, drink, and have a good time with their friends during the April Fair. Outsiders are welcome, unless it's up to the hilt. Sometimes, the *caseta* is so hospitable that money is not accepted. In that case, the outsider should behave as a guest of the house.

Millions of coloured-paper Chinese lanterns decorate the fairground streets. This tradition was brought from Italy in 1860.

The April Fair goes back in history to the old livestock fairs that have been held in the city since time immemorial. A Catalan, Narciso Bonaplata, and a Basque, Count Ybarra, changed it during the reign of Isabella II, turning it into an ephemeral city to celebrate the arrival of spring.

At the Fair, people drink dry *fino* sherry and *manzanilla* to combat the heat and to tone up their voices for singing. If you're thirsty, gazpacho. And you eat the same as always: fried fish the first night, and the rest of the time, much choice ham, sharp cheese, chickpea stew, potato omelette, and breaded fillets. Eating is done little by little together with much wine and dance, and in different *casetas* with different people. A good cup of broth goes down well at any hour because it tones you up. In the early morning, on the way home, there are *buñuelos* and chocolate that the Gypsy *casetas* traditionally serve during Seville's April Fair.

The popular **Calle del Infierno**—Hell Street—is a riotous amusement park that is set up next to the fairground for both children and grown-ups to have a good time. It is so loud that the Sevillians gave it its present name.

El Rocío

After the April Fair, thousands of Sevillians get ready to participate in the Rocío pilgrimage, which is the most popular of the Andalusian pilgrimages. Many *broth-*

erhoods leave Seville on horseback or in carts drawn by oxen or mules. At their front is the *simpecado*, a banner in honour of the Virgin that is carried on a beautiful wooden or silver cart. The road to El Rocío passes close to Doñana, and the nights are exceptional. In the village of El Rocío, in the midst of the marshes nature area, merriment and devotion become one and the same.

La Velá de Santa Ana

Around Saint Anne's day, the 26th of July, the old seafaring district of Triana celebrates the festival of its patron saint with a traditional soiree with the Guadalquivir River as witness.

In 1570, Governor Don Fadrique Enriquez de Ribera, on his way back from the Holy Land, brought to Seville a procession based on Jesus' road to Calvary. He had a sign put on the façade of the Casa de Pilatos—"Pilate's House" •*110*—that marked the beginning of the Stations of the Cross.

HOLY WEEK

Holy Week is Seville's great festival and is both famous and popular. Dating from the 14th century, it took its style from the Seville Baroque period. The form of the floats and the penitents' attire was influenced by the Romantic style. Each day of Holy Week, seven or eight religious brotherhoods make their *penitence station* and take the floats out onto the street accompanied by thousands of penitents. In the presence of such an accumulation of religiosity, art, and emotions, the Sevillians experience a very special week.

The oldest brotherhoods are Silence (*left*) founded in 1340, and Vera Cruz, founded in 1370. In the 16th century, the owners of the ships that travelled to the New World founded the Mount Zion Brotherhood. The most popular brotherhoods nowadays have thousands of brothers and are committed to observing the rules that are previously approved by the Church. However, besides being a spiritual matter, belonging to a brotherhood is a tradition that is part of family heritage.

The brotherhoods parade in *cofradías* along a specific route and with a fixed schedule. They leave the neighbourhood church, follow the official circuit, which includes going through the Cathedral, and then return home. The Guide Cross goes first, then the penitents, and finally the float and a band. There are two floats in almost all of the *cofradías*. The first one carries a statue of Christ, and the statue of the Virgin Mary follows. The circuit around the neighbourhood and entering the church are the best parts of the route. These are announced in the daily press and in numerous brochures.

The bands play weii-known processional marches such as *Amargura*, the Holy Week hymn. The author, Manuel Font de Anta, was inspired to compose it by this photograph in Paris in 1919. Another famous march, *Los Campanilleros*, has an ancestral prohibition that the Virgen de la Macarena likes to ignore.

There are penitents of all ages and from all walks of life. The brothers must take out their reservation ticket ahead of time, and they have their tunic, cape, conical hood, and sash made in the traditional establishments of the city. In some *cofradías*, such as *La Candelaria*, almost half of the penitents are women.

La madrugá is Seville's night-time. The Maundy Thursday processions finish when the early morning ones are going out. The latter ones run into the Good Friday processions. The Macarena, with three thousand penitents, sets off at midnight and they don't let it enter until two in the afternoon. Thousands of Sevillians also want to see the Esperanza de Triana, the Gran Poder, the Gitanos, the Cachorro… So special is this night in Seville that it has an ecclesiastical dispensation to disregard the traditional fasting and abstinence observed by Christians on Good Friday.

The Lord of Seville is Nuestro Padre Jesús del Gran Poder, a masterful carving by Juan de Mesa. Seeing its image reflected on the walls of the Plaza del Museo •97 is very moving.

The **saeta** is a brief and sententious song that adds a note of infinite tenderness and deep religious emotion to Holy Week. The throaty voice of the *cantaor* issues unexpectedly from any balcony in honour of the image that is passing. The voices of the best *cantaores* (*left: Antonio Mairena*) have been heard on the streets of Seville during Holy Week, and today it is possible to hear *saeteros* such as Angelita Yruela, who usually sings when *La Paz* goes through María Luisa Park • *148*, or Peregil, who sings when the *Cachorro* enters its church • *133*, or Antoñita Moreno, who sings when the *Baratillo* • *130* returns home. The entrance of the *Gitanos* brotherhood at the Church of San Román • *115* is a veritable *saeta* festival: couplet after couplet arise amid the audience, sometimes overlapping, with the throatiest voices lingering most.

The relationship between the *Gitanos* brotherhood and the House of Alba is widely known in Seville. A member of this family is a *costalero* or bearer for one of the floats. It is therefore very moving to watch this float pass in front of the Palacio de las Dueñas • *121*.

The *Macarena* is one of the most popular floats for the people of Seville. They say that the Virgin laughs or cries, depending on how you look at her. And it is clear that she always goes home with a *tired* face, a sensation that comes from the soot of the candles and the noon-time sun. The best place to see her pass by is Calle Parras • *119*, where Tía Marta or Manuel Mairena usually sing to her. Manuel Mairena has the consent of his brotherhood, the *Gitanos*, to sing to the Macarena here, from Juanita Reina's balcony. The emeralds and diamonds that the Virgin wears on her bosom were a gift from the bullfighter Joselito el Gallo.

The most representative image by Martínez Montañés, *Pasión*, is one of Jesus of Nazareth with measured features and perfect proportions. They say that its sculptor followed it through the streets marvelling that such a work of art could come from his hands. Do not miss it at the Plaza del Salvador entering its temple • *91*.

The *Esperanza de Triana*, rides on a float in pure Triana style. With her motherly face and dark complexion, she is most moving when being paraded around the neighbourhood, above all before Saint Anne's • *131*

During the Peninsular War against Napoleon, the Central *Junta* of the National Government is established in Seville (1810). The country's first steam vessel is built at the city's shipyards, and social unrest leads to the growth of banditry. The School of Bullfighting is created in the San Bernardo district. Gustavo Adolfo Bécquer writes his *Rimas y Leyendas*. Isabella II finances some important works: the Triana bridge and the Plaza Nueva. The April Fair is held for the first time. The Duke and Duchess of Montpensier set up their 'little Court' in Seville, at the Palacio de San Telmo, currently the seat of the Andalusian regional government. During the First Republic, Seville proclaims itself an independent canton and a Federal Constitution for Andalusia is planned. The newspaper *El Correo de Andalucía*, now Seville's oldest daily, is founded in 1898.

Los duques de
Montpensier

Work is also done on floats and platforms for the Holy Week processions, for which cedar, white pine, Guatemala cedar, and mahogany is used. A traditional part of the artistic work of woodcraft is the coffered ceiling. It was the Mudejar influence, with its geometric tracery, which gave rise to its final form.

The manufacture of horse-drawn carriages is a centuries-old tradition. Workshops in Seville, Carmona, Alcalá de Guadaira, and Dos Hermanas today restore carriages such as light barouches, phaetons, spider phaetons, charres, broughams, galeras, dogcarts, peters, landaus, calashes, char-a-bancs, berlins, sociables, omnibuses and *chavalas*. In this work, they use oak wood, holm oak, poplar, and acacia.

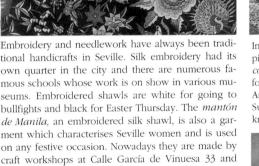

The float of the Virgen de los Angeles has a peculiar Neo-Byzantine style with a cloak of angels carved out of ivory. Its brotherhood, the *Negritos*, gave admission to the first white man halfway through the last century, three hundred years after its founding. The best place to see it is Plaza de la Alfalfa • *109*.

El Cachorro. This is a 17th-century Baroque image of Christ carved out of cedar. Its sculptor was inspired by the face of a dying Gypsy who was stabbed, according to legend, on the Triana bridge. It is even more moving under the Postigo del Aceite • *129*.

Gastronomy. The people of Seville have a peculiar way of understanding this religious festival, in which merriment and spirit are never lacking. It is an occasion to taste in any place some good *torrijas* or *pestiños* (honey fritters), familiar sweets from the era of al-Andalus, made with honey and spices such as aniseed. And at lunchtime, Holy Week stew, yellow and with hard-boiled egg, and also codfish with tomato.

The candle-making trade has maintained its standing in Seville thanks to Holy Week. All sorts of candles—*cirios, velas, bujías*—including elaborate floral candles are manufactured using virgin wax and paraffin. After blending both products, the candles are made by dipping the wicks into the vat. Then, they are weighed, calibrated, cut, and, if necessary, dyed.

A considerable number of Sevillian woodworking craftsmen make floats and platforms from cedar, white pine, Guatemala cedar, and mahogany. Very little machinery is used and some of these craftsmen make exquisite wood carvings.

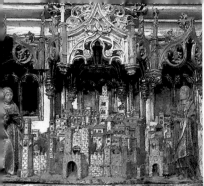

IMAGE MAKING

Seville is the main centre for traditional Spanish image making, which saw its golden age in the 16th c. when the main altarpiece of the cathedral was made • 72 (section shown on left). Martínez Montañés, influenced by Torrigiani and drawing on Seville's heritage from previous centuries, created a definitive school that was consolidated by his disciples Juan de Mesa and Alonso Cano, all of whom are, together with Pedro Roldán, Juan de Astorga, F. Antonio Gijón, and Ocampo, authors of many of Seville's Holy Week images (17th c.). The great image maker of the 20th c. is Castillo Lastrucci. Today, more than thirty prestigious artisans work in image making in Seville. Images are usually carved from cedar and sometimes from ivory. The task is far from easy: drawings and sketches, and then a clay model must be made. Measurements and form are transferred to wood with a device invented by Leonardo da Vinci. Here is where the work of a master carver begins. Clay is applied with a paintbrush on the

wood carvings, and then they are gilded with extremely thin gold leaf. Finally, the images are dressed to make the outlines and reliefs stand out. Curiously enough egg yolk is used in this process.

Since the 15th century, Seville has been the main centre for **embroidery** for Holy Week. It is an embroidery done with gold and silver threads, silk, velvet, and satin. This is a handicraft that requires only a needle and an embroidery frame. The history of this craft is full of the names of illustrious embroiderers that exported their work to all parts of the world, especially to the Americas and India. When it is applied to the capes of the Virgin and the covers of the baldachins, the craft becomes an art (a section of the cape of the Esperanza de Triana is shown above •48). There are several workshops in Seville that practice this craft nowadays. The embroidery of the cape, baldachin, and flies of the Amargura float is an unsurpassed work of art.

THE MAY CROSSES

The 'May Crosses' is an Andalusian tradition rooted in Seville since the 18th century. The residents of the most popular districts use Chinese lanterns and flowerpots to decorate the crosses that they set up in quiet plazas and public areas or in their own yards and patios. There they pass the evening with song, dance, and wine. These celebrations are at the weekends during the month of May and are advertised in the press.

It is also a tradition for the children to build miniature floats, which they later decorate and carry through the streets.

THE PROCESSIONS OF GLORY

Between the months of May and November, many *Glory Brotherhoods* parade through the streets of Seville, surprising the passersby. The cycle begins on the second Sunday of May with the *Glory Proclamation* in the Placita de los Naranjos at El Salvador Basilica • 91, and by the parading of the ancient image of the Virgen de la Salud, which belongs to an 18th-century brotherhood.

CORPUS CHRISTI

The festivity of Corpus Christi, the Thursday of the eighth week after Easter Sunday, is one of the city's great days. As in Granada and Toledo, it is a holiday. The procession of the Holy Sacrament (carried in an excellent monstrance wrought by Juan de Arfe) leaves the cathedral very early and makes a brief but intense circuit through the most central streets of the city. The fragrance given off by the rosemary that has been strewn as a carpet along the route of the procession, and the altars that the Sevillians place on corners and bends, create a very characteristic atmosphere. It is worthwhile taking a look at the shop windows on the streets along the way, especially Calle Francos •_90_ and Calle Sierpes • _95_, decorated with Baroque motifs for the occasion. The balconies wear their best finery, shawls, and embroidery, and the women usually go with white shawls.

"Tres jueves hay en Sevilla / que relumbran más que el sol, / Jueves Santo, Corpus Christi / y el día de la Ascensión"

The dance of the **Seises** is one of the oldest traditions in the city, and one of its most peculiar sights. There are records of these dances dating back to the 15th century, and they are performed by children who dance and sing before the Holy Sacrament under an ancient papal bull. They sing old medieval carols, galliards, jigs, and pavanes to the rhythm of castanets. They wear a garb in the style of the court of the Habsburgs—with jerkin, knee breeches, and a feathered hat, garments that have always been the same since the time of Archbishop Palafox. This Archbishop was so insistent on putting a stop to the custom, because he found it disrespectful to sing and dance, with their hats on, before the Holy Sacrament, that he went to the Pope. The Pope, not wanting to contradict the prelate, decided to allow it but *only as long as the present garments lasted*. Since the one who makes the law creates the loophole, this ruling was joyfully accepted by the people of Seville, who decided not to substitute the clothes with new ones ever again but to repair them. This has been done ever since. The *Seises* accompany the monstrance during the Corpus procession and sing and dance when they reach the altars set up in the Plaza de San Francisco •_93_ and Plaza del Salvador •_92_. They also dance before the main altar of the cathedral •_66_ during the eight days following this festivity, and during the eight days' period after the Immaculate Conception (8 December).

CHRISTMAS

Christmas in Seville has a series of religious and cultural traditions that have been adapted to the different courses that history has taken. It is, without a doubt, a peculiar Christmas celebration in which it can be seen, once again, that Seville is the capital of the south. The city is flooded with nativity and manger scenes set up by churches, associations, and brotherhoods. A list is published each year in the press and they are visited by thousands of people.

The **villancico** is an ancient popular song that comes from the *zéjel* and has its roots in the Andalusian countryside. They can be performed by a polyphonic choir, by a *campanilleros* or bell-ringing choir, by a group of friends, or in a *tango* or *bulería* style in any town of Andalusia. By tradition, the *campanilleros* go out onto the streets around Christmas, and they create a very special Christmas atmosphere. When singing *villancicos*, the musicians keep a slow and constant rhythm using bells, triangles, graters, tambourines, zambombas, and earthenware jars played with a hemp sandal. They are accompanied by a guitar.

Inmaculada, Bartolomé Esteban Murillo, 17th century

SEVILLE FINE ARTS MUSEUM •98

This is the second picture gallery in Spain after the Prado Museum, and it holds works from top-ranking artists with universal names from the Seville School: Murillo, Velázquez, Zurbarán, Pacheco, Valdés Leal…

St. Jerome
Pietro Torrigiani,
16th century

This sculpture inspired the masters of religious image-making in Seville, which is the artistic key to the famous Holy Week. The world is full today of important works by these masters: Juan Martínez Montañés, Pedro Roldán, Juan de Mesa, Juan de Astorga, Francisco Antonio Gijón…

St. Bruno,
Juan Martínez Montañés, 17th century.
Seville Fine Arts Museum.
Sculpture made of polychrome wood.

Portrait of Jorge Manuel Theotokópoulos,
El Greco.
Seville Fine Arts Museum.

The Cigar Girls,
Gonzalo Bilbao.
Seville Fine Arts Museum.

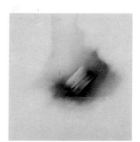

MUSEUM OF MODERN ART

Santas Justa y Rufina, Goya.
Cathedral.

This painting of the patron saints of the city is kept within the walls of **Seville Cathedral,** one of the countless works of art that are on display here • *66*.

This museum is on Calle Santo Tomás and houses an interesting collection of contemporary Spanish art, including works by Tàpies, César Manrique, Fernando Zóbel (*top*) and the Sevillian Luis Gordillo (*bottom*).

THE PAVILION OF NAVIGATION

This is an attractive sample of the seafaring history of Seville offered to the visitor with the aid of advanced technological means. It is one of the Pavilions of the Universal Exposition that can be visited on the Isla de la Cartuja: the most up-to-date museum in the city, which shows the relationship of Seville with the sea • *137*.

THE ARCHAEOLOGICAL MUSEUM

This museum houses the foremost collection of ancient art from southern Spain. Tartessians, Phoenicians and Romans settled in Andalusia and left behind objects of extraordinary interest. Here you can see the El Carambolo Treasure, dating from the 7th century BC. It is a man's set of jewels decorated with pure gold hemispheres, rosettes, and cords. It is said that they are the jewels of Arganthonius, king of the Tartessians • *150*.

THE FOLK ARTS AND CUSTOMS MUSEUM

This museum provides an interesting sample of different aspects of Seville culture: life-size models of the rooms and outbuildings of a noble house and a rural house, furniture, old costumes, horse carriages, everyday utensils, models of local musical instrument workshops… and the best collection of historical April Fair posters • *150*. This museum and the Archaeological Museum are both on the Plaza de América in María Luisa Park • *148*.

The best-known **Art Galleries** are those of *Juana de Aizpuru* (Calle Zaragoza 26), *Marta Moore* (Calle Velarde 96), *La Máquina Española* (Plaza Cristo de Burgos 5), or *Fausto Velázquez* (Calle San Isidoro 4).

Seville has other museums of interest, such as the Archive of the Indies • *77* *(above)*, where the documents of the New World are kept, the Naval Museum at the Tower of Gold • *126*, the museum and ruins at Italica, the Museum of the Royal Equestrian Society • *127*, the Hospital-Museum of Charity • *128*, the treasure of Jesús del Gran Poder • *101* and of La Virgen de la Macarena • *117*, the house of the Countess of Lebrija • *92*, the Casa de Pilatos • *110*, and the Palacio de las Dueñas • *121*.

55

MARKETS AND FLEA MARKETS
El Jueves is the traditional flea market that has existed in Seville since the 14th century. It sets up along Calle Feria • *120* and takes place on Thursday mornings. It is a bustling, old-fashioned flea market where traders and hawkers, peddlers and junk dealers sell everything: antiques, old clothes, knick-knacks, stamp collections and religious pictures. Another traditional flea market is the one held at **Alfalfa** • *109* on Sunday mornings, in which all kinds and species of pets can be acquired. The flea market at **El Cabildo** • *77* also takes place on Sunday mornings. Here, philatelists and numismatists rub shoulders with card collectors and cigar-band collectors, and mingle with enthusiasts and curious onlookers. Knick-knacks and old junk are also sold on Sundays in the **Alameda de Hércules** • *105*.

As for markets, there are some really attractive ones in Seville, such as the one on Calle Feria • *119* *(above)* from the 17th century, or the quiet markets of Osuna • *158* and Estepa • *159*.

TRANSPORTATION

The AVE is the fastest high-speed train in Europe and links Seville with the capital of Spain in less that two and a half hours. The city is also linked directly by air with the main cities of Europe; a new network of motorways and main roads connects Seville with the centre and periphery of the country. Seville's port is the only inland port in Spain and handles both tourist cruises and regular freight line traffic. Since Spain joined the EU, it is classified as a European cabotage port, mainly because of its specific characteristics: an inland port with an eighty-kilometre-long navigable estuary with a depth of around 6 metres and a tidal range of 2 metres that permits traffic of medium-sized ships of 10,000 gross tonnes. Visiting ships can tie up at Las Delicias Quay, right in the heart of the city.

THE MEDIA

The city has an international press centre, equipped with the most up-to-date communications technology for the use of information professionals. The main studios of the regional television station, Canal Sur, and the Andalusian regional centre of TVE, the Spanish state television company, are in Seville. Numerous local radio stations can be

tuned into in Seville, and all of the national networks have their regional offices here. The city newspapers are *El Correo de Andalucía, ABC,* and *Diario 16 Andalucía* (which prints a special edition for Seville). *El País* has its regional office here and publishes an Andalusian section daily. Other national publications such as the daily *El Mundo* and the magazine *Tiempo* also have offices here.

THE SUMMER CINEMA

Although in Seville there are a good number of cinemas and theatres, the most idiosyncratic ones are these peculiar open-air patios where films are shown on summer nights. The smell of dama de noche, jasmine, and recently-watered *albero* earth is consubstan-

tial with the summer cinema. The visitor always has a choice 'icebox' at his disposal where they offer popular *tapas* of potato omelette and *papas aliñás* or garnished potatoes. Some of the more noteworthy are the oldest surviving summer cinema (Calle Pagés del Corro) and the most modern one, built in a very traditional style for the 1992 Universal Exposition and located on the Isla de la Cartuja.

PLACES OF INTEREST

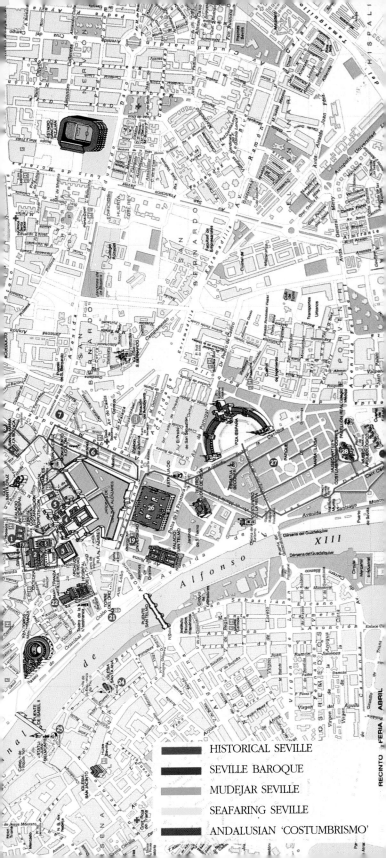

HISTORICAL SEVILLE

SEVILLE BAROQUE

MUDEJAR SEVILLE

SEAFARING SEVILLE

ANDALUSIAN 'COSTUMBRISMO'

The old quarter of Seville is one of the largest in Europe, and practically all of it is worth visiting. In addition to this area, the historical district of Triana *(the other Seville)* and the Isla de la Cartuja to one side of the Guadalquivir, and the historic city built during the first half of the century on the other side make a one-day visit to Seville practically impossible. However, circumstances oblige us all, and the traveller even more. Therefore, the visitor is recommended in this case to check the General Index of Places in this book • *168*. He should also go over the following itinerary, pearls chosen with different criteria so that, in spite of its brevity, the jewel does not los its fullness.

Start your tour very early, leaving from the Giralda (which is worth climbing to obtain a panoramic view of the city and to situate oneself) • *65*. Visit the Cathedral, making sure to pay special attention to the main altar, the choir loft and retrochoir, and the royal chapel • *66*. From here, continue to the Alcazar • *78*, later taking a short walk through the Santa Cruz district • *82*. When you get back to the Giralda once again, you can take Calle Francos • *90* and enter the lively commercial city around El Salvador • *92*, Plaza de San Francisco • *93*, and Calle Sierpes • *95*.

You can spend the evening along the Guadalquivir (which you reach after crossing the centre of the city on the Avenida de la Constitución). Riverside Seville can be broken down into four parts: the Puerta de Jerez • *128*, the Paseo de Colón • *125*, María Luisa Park • *148*, and the Isla de la Cartuja • *134*. What a good day it will be if you happen to finish in the Triana district, where you will witness an unforgettable nightfall.

Historical Seville

SEVILLE, THE CITY

In this first circuit that we are proposing to the reader, you will visit the Seville of the many cultures. The city is the result of the settlement of the greatest civilizations in the history of the Western Hemisphere, and you will be able to verify this as you follow this itinerary where, besides the Roman and Visigothic ruins that you can see up close, you will be witness to the supreme works of later cultures, such as the Moslem Giralda, the Gothic Cathedral, the Mudejar Alcazar, or the two Jewish quarters of Seville. An accumulation of different contrasts define this city once and for all as a universal city.

The Giralda area. The Plaza Virgen de los Reyes is the heart of old Seville, with the Giralda, the Patio de los Naranjos, and the Cathedral to one side, and the portal of the

Archbishop's Palace on the other side. This portal is one of the best of the Seville Baroque style. The colours of the building, bull's-blood red and *albero* yellow, stand out and characterize palatial facades in Seville. It is worthwhile taking a look at the main staircase and the 16th-century fountain in the second patio. Across from the palace, you can see the eternal cypress and the white silhouette of the **Convento de la Encarnación**. In its church, which was the chapel of the old hospital of Santa Marta, you can still see abundant remains of the building erected in 1385. Very nearby, along a narrow, sinuous street, you come upon the beautiful **Placita de Santa Marta**, a pool of peace and beauty, with a cross that used to indicate the boundary of the old San Lázaro Hospital, and which was brought here later. You can take a walk under the orange trees of Calle Mateos Gago until you reach the passageway formed by two houses built by the regionalist architects Talavera and Espiau. The Café Giralda is halfway down the street. Here you can have breakfast or try exquisite *tapas* in what used to be a Moorish bathhouse.

Five metres up the facade of the Giralda that faces the Plaza Virgen de los Reyes, you can see a niche with a Baroque Virgin made of white marble. This is the *Virgen de los Olmos*, who used to preside the plenary sessions when the former city hall, known as the Corral de los Olmos, used to stand next to the Giralda.

The tower of the Giralda is the minaret of the main mosque of Seville, which was destroyed in the 15th century to build the Cathedral. The construction of the tower was begun in the year 1184 under the rule of the Abbasid Abu Yacub Yusuf. The ceremony of the crowning of the minaret took place fourteen years later when the tower was crowned with four huge golden balls of decreasing sizes, one above the other. These balls dazzled the Sevillians of the period with their rays for 150 years. It was the tallest tower of its time and was raised to mark the centre of the Almohad Empire. In 1356, an earthquake toppled the balls with a roar and, in 1400, after the city had been christianized, King Peter had a simple belfry installed. In 1558, the architect Hernán Ruiz transformed it with the construction of the bell tower section, now an essential part of its appearance. The Almohad tower thus became the symbol of the Christian faith and the symbol of Seville.

The Giralda is 97 metres high and can be climbed by means of 35 ramps, which made it possible for the muezzin to climb it on horseback to call the faithful to prayer with his song from the heights. This peculiarity makes it unique in the western world. Each one of the four sides of the tower is decorated with large panels of carved bricks *(sebka)* with windows framed by arches with a complex decoration.

The Renaissance-style bell tower section houses twenty-five bells of all ages. The oldest one, the one of the clock, is the only one that does not have a name; it was cast in 1400. Nineteen of them have a clapper and can peal, and six have hammers and are used for tolling. One of them, Santa María, weighs six tons, and another, San Cristóbal, had to be recast because it recently took flight and landed flat on the Patio de los Naranjos. In the *Rules and Order* for ringing the bells of the Giralda, special series are established, such as the one for 'hangings' (1533) and, a century later, the one for 'deaths of popes and kings'.

The tower gets its name from the **_giraldillo_**, the weather vane in the shape of a Renaissance woman that was installed after the Christian bell tower was built during the reign of Philip II. It is the work of Juan Bautista Vázquez the Elder, who also carved the well-known Cristo de Burgos, and the Cristo de los Manzipes at Tunja Cathedral in Colombia. Cast in bronze by Bartolomé Morell, the figure has a great deal of symbolism and in Seville is commonly known as Santa Juana because the general public confused it with Joan of Arc when the statue was taken down to the Corral de los Olmos many years ago.

SEVILLA, La Giralda y Patio de las Naranjo

The **Patio de los Naranjos** is, together with the Giralda, the only remains of the city's main mosque. It can be reached through the Puerta del Lagarto or Gate of the Lizard in the Plaza Virgen de los Reyes, or better, through the Puerta del Perdón (Calle Alemanes), with a splendid exterior portal that has sculptures and high reliefs by Miguel Florentín (early 16th century). The leaves of this door are covered with copper with decorations of lacery and Kufic inscriptions • 67. The knockers are from the Almohad period (12th century). For centuries, in the interior of the patio, the Sevillians performed ablutions as acts of purification. The design of the upper part of its central fountain is Visigothic and St. Hermenegild was baptized there. The irrigation channels that run through it continue to be a reminder of its earliest history. In 1618, its space was reduced to its present size when the sacrarium of the Cathedral was built, today the parish church of El Sagrario • 76. The Patio de los Naranjos preserves the pulpit from which three saints of the history of the Church preached. There are also a number of tombs among which you will see that of the Sevillians who preferred the scaffold rather than betray their fellow conspirators against Napoleon. It is held that the stuffed lizard that hangs in the gallery of the Columbian Library • 76 was a present from the Sultan of Egypt to Alfonso X the Wise.

Seville Cathedral is the largest cathedral by area in the world, according to the Guinness Book of Records. It has its origin in the ancient mosque of Seville, built in the 9th century by the Almohad King Abd ar-Rahman II, where the Byzantine Basilica of Saint Vincent was located. After the conquest of Seville by Ferdinand III (the Saint) in 1248, the city experienced a process of christianization and many of its mosques and minarets were converted into churches and bell towers. At the beginning of the 15th century, the destruction of the mosque was approved, and construction on the cathedral was begun under the supervision of Alonso Martínez. The works were finished a century later, but soon afterwards the roof caved in destroying for History countless works by Pedro Millán, Jorge Fernández, Sebastián de Almohacid, and Niculoso Pisano. In 1519, the master Gil de Ontañón inaugurated it after covering it with stone vaults, disdaining plans for a wooden roof as "too unsafe and sumptuous."

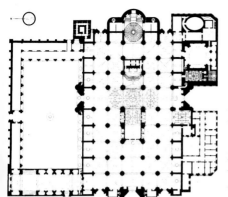

The Cathedral

It is the largest Gothic temple in the world. Its floor plan is square, consisting of five naves (the central one being wider) covered by seventy ogival vaults that are supported by forty piers, some of which are fifty-six metres tall. When its construction was ordered, they say that the Cathedral Chapter declared: "Let us build such a great work that those who see it finished will consider us mad." This is a worthy cathedral that would later oversee the episcopal seats of the New World.

Besides the Puerta del Perdón that gives access to the Patio de los Naranjos, the cathedral can be entered through other doors, of which the most beautiful are perhaps those of Palos and of Campanillas, located at the sanctuary side (Plaza Virgen de los Reyes). These are splendid works with terra-cotta tympanums by Miguel Florentín in 1520. The two small doors located opposite (Avenida de la Constitución) are also exceptional and were built a little earlier by Lorenzo Mercadante and Pedro Millán.

The interior of the Cathedral is usually reached through the Puerta de los Palos (Plaza Virgen de los Reyes). Walk through from left to right and take a look at its many chapels that have held countless artistic works for centuries. Leave the choir and the main chapel in the central nave for last, where you can see the main altarpiece, crowning work of Sevillian art. Now, you can see in the first place to the left **Saint Peter's Chapel**, which has a majestic altarpiece painted by Zurbarán in 1625.

From there, go to the **Royal Chapel**, situated at the sanctuary side of the Cathedral, passing through a wrought-iron grille financed by Charles III and crowned by a curious group of sculptures that shows King Ferdinand (the Saint) receiving the vassalage of Axafat, the last Moorish king of Seville. Built in 1551 in a pure Renaissance style, its clarity and plateresque or even Mannerist decoration contrasts with the rest of the Gothic chapels. The image of the Virgen de los Reyes, patron of Seville, is in the centre of the altar (*Per me reges regnant*, kings reign for me). The image was carved from larch wood in the 13th century; the hair, simulated with threads of silk and gold, is outstanding. An elaborately worked windowed silver case by Laureano de Pina (17th century) contains the uncorrupted remains of the patron saint of the city, Saint Ferdinand • _28_, which are put on public display when his day is celebrated on 30 May. The altar also safeguards the image of the *Virgen de las Batallas*, carved out of ivory, and which is of unmistakably French workmanship and is the first vestige of the religious imagery of Ferdinand's time. It was the image that accompanied the Saint-King onto the field of battle. In the side walls of the chapel are the sepulchres of Alfonso X the Wise and his mother, Beatrice of Swabia. The remains of King Peter are also in this chapel.

Saint Michael's Chapel now contains the famous *Cristo de la Clemencia*, one of the major works of the Seville Baroque religious imagery, sculpted by Martínez Montañés in 1603. The image is from the Monastery of Santa María de las Cuevas • *134* and is the prototype of the Andalusian Christ, free of wounds and blood. The *Virgen del Buen Aire* has been placed beside it temporarily. She, with a schooner in her hands, is the patron saint of navigators and is from the Palacio de San Telmo • *142*, formerly a nautical college.

Beside the Puerta de Campanillas, there is a delicate group of sculptures by Duque Cornejo that represents the saints of Seville, Justa and Rufina. In the south nave, is the **Capilla del Mariscal**, or Field Marshal's Chapel, which contains an altarpiece that is the best surviving work by Pedro de Campaña. From here, you can reach other rooms in the Cathedral and you can visit them later.

The former mihrab of the mosque was in what is now the **Capilla de la Virgen de la Antigua**. Curiously, Cardinal Hurtado de Mendoza wanted to be buried here following the Moslem tradition. The image of the Virgin that presides the chapel is an icon painted alfresco according to the Byzantine custom. The cardinal's mausoleum is one of the earliest works from the Spanish Renaissance period.

At the right end of the transept, next to the Puerta de San Cristóbal, is the grandiose tomb where the remains of Christopher Columbus supposedly lie. Although it was designed towards the end of the last century for Havana cathedral, it remained in Seville after Cuba gained independence.

Next is the **Capilla de la Gamba**, with a fine altarpiece by Luis de Vargas in which the perfection of Adam's leg has always impressed people (that is the explanation for the Italian word that gives the chapel its name).

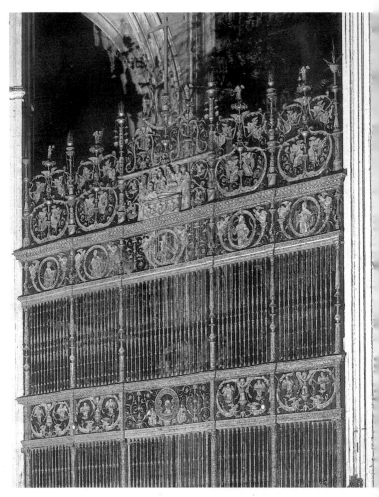

The **Main Chapel**, where the wedding of HRH Princess Elena de Borbón and Dor
Jaime de Marichalar took place, has the largest altarpiece in all Christendom, a perfec
work of decoration and iconography constructed in the 15th century and to which th
most important sculptors of the period made their contributions. The *Virgen de la Sed*
(13th century), made of carved and embossed silver imitating textile motifs, preside
over the chapel. The pulpits are made of wrought iron by Francisco Salamanca (15t
century). The massive grille was erected in the 16th century •*72 and* •*73*.

In the **Choir** *(above)* the ebony choir stalls, carved in a florid Gothic style with Mudejar traces, are the leading feature. Note also the splendid Renaissance lectern and the organ, a genuine work of art that has known the sensibility of the foremost organists. In the retrochoir there is a wealth of jasper and bronze, in the mannerist style, and on the southern side of the choir, a small chapel houses the popular *Virgen Cieguecita*, an Immaculate Conception with half-closed eyes sculpted by Martínez Montañés.

In the **Chapel of the Bishop of Scala** is the bishop's empty tomb and the relief of the *Virgen de la Granada (right)*, in polychrome terra-cotta, by the Florentine sculptor Andrea della Robbia. There is another Virgin by this author on the wall of the nearby **St. James' Chapel**, on whose altarpiece there are paintings by Roelas and Valdés Leal.

The *Vision of St. Anthony,* one of the most important paintings by Bartolomé Esteban Murillo, presides the altarpiece of the **Baptismal Chapel**.

The Cathedral's stained-glass windows were made by the most famous artists in Europe (Arnao de Flandes, Carlos de Brujas, Enrique Alemán, Arnao de Vergara), creating a style and a great glassworking tradition.

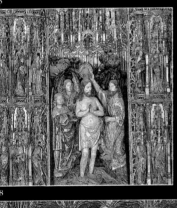

CATHEDRAL MAIN ALTARPIECE AND DETAILS

1.- PRAYERS IN THE GARDEN

2.- THE THREE MARYS BEFORE THE SEPULCHRE

3.- THE *VIRGEN DOLOROSA*

4.- ST JOHN EVANGELIST

5.- THE NATIVITY OF OUR LORD

6.- THE ORIGINAL SIN

7.- TRANSFIGURATION

8.- THE BAPTISM

9.- ON THE WAY TO CALVARY

10.- THE ASCENSION OF OUR LORD

The **Main Sacristy** can be entered through a chapel that has a stained-glass window by Arnao de Flandes and some cabinets with reliefs, the work of Duque Cornejo. There is also a painting by Zurbarán. Accessed through an oblique arch, the interior of the sacristy is a notable enclosure designed by Diego de Riaño and laid out as a Greek cross. The entire space is decorated with rich, sculptured ornamentation organized in terms of the front wall from which three chapels open out. In the hall, there are paintings by Murillo (St. Isidore and St. Leander *top*) Zurbarán, Lucas Jordán, Alonso Vázquez… and reliquaries and chests of great artistic value, together with the famous 13th-century **Alphonsine Tables,** one of the most representative medieval Spanish silver works: a triptych made of embossed, gold-plated silver with a wealth of emeralds and amethysts, and agate cameos. The other item of great value in this hall is the monumental **Monstrance**, one of the biggest in Christendom, made by Juan de Arfe. This jewel weighs over three hundred kilograms and is one of the outstanding works of the Spanish Renaissance (16th century). One of the most important sculptures that can be found in this sacristy is that of St. Ferdinand

The Cathedral

by Pedro Roldán on a silver base (*below*).

The elliptical **Chapter House** is also by Hernán Ruiz. It has a clear Mannerist style, and you will notice the peculiar design of the flooring and the dome, which contains an exceptional series of pictures by Murillo presided over by an *Immaculate Conception*.

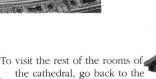

To visit the rest of the rooms of the cathedral, go back to the Capilla del Mariscal, which is located at the sanctuary side of the temple, in the south nave. From there, you can reach the antechamber, chapter house, and main sacristy. All these areas are of extraordinary architectural and artistic value and were built in the 16th century. Entrance is through the **Sala de Ornamentos,** or Ornament Room, which houses an outstanding sculpture of St. Joseph by Pedro Roldán (1664), together with a collection of richly artistic ornaments such as the popular *Pendón de San Fernando* and the *Terliz de la Montería.*

The **Antechamber** is a rectangular hall designed by Hernán Ruiz, as was the Chapter patio. Books and choral codices are displayed on music stands and lecterns.

Over the Lizard Gallery, in the Patio de los Naranjos, you will find the **Columbian Library**, the most important 15th-century private collection of books. It was carefully compiled by Hernando Columbus, the son of the Discoverer. Tourist visits are not allowed, but justified research work can be done.

Elio Antonio de Nebrija

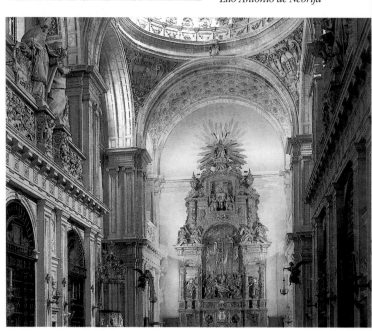

The cathedral's **Sacrarium,** today an independent parish church, was built in the 17th century, covering up a large part of the Patio de los Naranjos. The cathedral's Capilla de la Granada, where Elio Antonio de Nebrija spoke, was also located here. (Nebrija wrote the first Spanish grammar.) The Sacrarium is worth visiting, above all to see the Baroque splendour of the main altarpiece, which used to be in the former Convent of San Francisco on the Plaza Nueva, •*94*. It can be reached from the Avenida de la Constitución. The sculptures by Pedro Roldán, for example his *Descent from the Cross* and the altarpieces of the lateral wings of the temple, carved by Duque Cornejo, are astounding. The supreme beauty of the wall tiling in the sacristy is also surprising.

Going outside again to the Avenida de la Constitución and circling the Cathedral on your left, you can see a flat, square building with large paired pilasters at the four corners of the building. This is the **Archive of the Indies**, built as a commodity exchange by Philip II, where the commercial treaties with the New World were signed during the first two centuries following the Discovery. The archive holds the most important collection of documents on that crucial historical period, which are now being digitised through a state-of-the-art computer system. Today, over fifteen million pages of documents stored within these walls can be looked up from anywhere in the world.

Crossing the Avenida de la Constitución, across from the main facade of the Cathedral, you will enter, through the **Pasaje de los Seises,** the small and completely renovated **Plaza Interior del Cabildo**, where there are still remains of the Roman city wall. In a small shop, you will be able to buy sweets from Seville's convents • *31* or, if it is a Sunday morning, take in the peculiar atmosphere created by the old flea market of antique coins and stamps. In this place, which was the canonical school of San Miguel, Juan de Arfe wrought his famous monstrance and Hilarión Eslava composed his well-known *Miserere*.

If you go around the Archive of the Indies along the facade of the Cathedral you will find, in the **Plaza del Triunfo**, the small memorial or 'triumph' set up in thanksgiving for the negligible damage that was caused in Seville by the 1755 Lisbon earthquake. In the centre of the plaza, there is an *Inmaculada* from the regionalist period. It is a sculpted copy of the original painted by Murillo for the Hospital de los Venerables, which was stolen by Napoleon and is now on display in the Louvre in Paris. The plaza is surrounded by the walls of the Alcazar and by a Baroque palace that is the property of the Seville Provincial Council.

The **Alcazar** is the premier palace of the city of Seville, historical apex of the different cultures that spread from here all over the Occident. The Roman Acropolis was on this ground, and over it, a great Visigothic basilica was built. There are remains of a fortified castle, and, from the very start, it was the central palace of the various Moorish dynasties. The conquering king died here, and the Spanish monarchy has always had a royal residence here, a tradition that continues today. Visiting the Alcazar is like stepping into history to observe the symbiosis.

The visit. From the Plaza del Triunfo, you can reach the Alcazar through the Puerta del León, or Lion's Gate. To the left, you will see the **Hall of Justice**, which was built by Alfonso XI and has the oldest Mudejar coffered ceiling in the palace. From there, go out to the **Patio de la Montería**, or Court of Venery, presided by the majestic facade of the **Palace of Peter I**. It is a unique 14th-century building, constructed by architects from Seville, Granada, and Toledo and by others sent by the Nasrid King Muhammad V. The mixture of cultures is evident in the workmanship of the arches, friezes, and lintels.

The interior of the palace shows two very different environments: the official area, and the family area. The first area gravitates around the **Patio de las Doncellas** or Court of the Maidens •*17*, which has the most beautiful wall tiling in the Alcazar, laid during the time of the Catholic Monarchs. From here, you move on to the three halls called the Bedroom, Charles V, and the **Hall of the Ambassadors.** The latter is the most important, and the most spectacular one in the palace: a square structure with a series of triple arches along the sides, covered with an interlaced dome on squinches and covered with stalactite decoration.

You then go to the Hall of the Philip II Ceiling, with a splendid stuccowork decoration, and then on to the private area of the Alcazar. The **Patio de las Muñecas**, or Court of the Dolls •*17* is in the centre. This patio is small and has a collection of capitals that support the arches. Adjoining are the **Hall of the Prince**, with an interesting coffered ceiling by Juan de Simancas, and the Bedroom of the Moorish Kings, behind some magnificent Mudejar doors decorated with laceries and vegetal motifs.

On the upper floor of the building, you can see the tilework altar made by the ceramist Niculoso Pisano in 1504 for the oratory of the Catholic Monarchs. The remaining rooms cannot normally be visited, as they are currently a residence of the Royal Family.

From the Patio de la Montería, you enter the **Cuarto del Almirante**, or Admiral's Room, decorated with tapestries by Goya, and the **Sala de Audiencias**, or Presence Chamber presided over by an altarpiece that shows the famous *Virgen de los Navegantes*, by Alejo Fernández. Also from the same patio, you can go to the Jardín del Crucero, also called the garden of María de Padilla, and enter the rooms of Charles V after crossing an excellent portal by Van der Borcht. This is now the area of the Alcazar of Alfonso X the Wise and in the **Chapel** you will be surprised by a painting of the *Virgen de la Antigua* and by excellent wall tiling. The adjoining **Salón de Tapices,** or Hall of Tapestries, holds the rich examples woven by the Royal Factory according to the design of the Dutchman Pannemaker. In the following rooms, you will see the wall tiling by the ceramist Cristóbal de Augusta (16th century).

Underneath the palace, you will find the **baths of doña María de Padilla**, King Peter's lover. It is a gallery of Gothic vaults built over the former Almohad garden. They say that the king invited his courtiers to drink of the water when Doña María was bathing. One who was summoned for refusing answered: "Sire, when I try the broth, I fancy the partridge."

However, a fundamental part of the Alcazar of Seville are the **Gardens**, full of enchantment and beauty, of the fragrances of plants and of the coolness that issues from the fountains. More than two hundred cedars, palm trees, cypresses, citrus trees, eucalyptuses, and oaks make up this botanical universe of mazes and gardens, in which there are also myrtles, jasmines, and damas de noche. The gardens closest to the building are Renaissance or Romantic in style with pools and Mannerist figures, such as the figure of Mercury by Diego de Pesquera, or the Galería del Grutesco, from which you will have a panoramic view of the different styles of the palace gardens. You will also see the Englishman's Garden, the Big Garden (with Neptune as a central fountain), and the Orange Grove Garden (with the Lion's basin)

Opposite is the **Pavilion of Charles V**, a square building decorated with wall tiling and stuccowork. Worth seeing is the vault by Juan Hernández (16th century) inside.

The Garden of the Alcubilla, which follows a Spanish-Moslem design and concept, is also known as the 'Tennis Courtyard' because Queen Victoria Eugenia set up the first tennis court in Spain on this spot.

You leave the Alcázar through the **Apeadero** built by Philip III in which you can see carriages and harnesses of the period. There, you will come upon a quiet spot called the Patio de Banderas, or Court of the Flags, the starting point of this circuit through Seville's Jewish quarter.

Seville's Jewish Quarter. Once Ferdinand the Saint had conquered the city, the second largest Jewish community in Spain (after the one in Toledo) settled in Seville. It had four synagogues (today they are churches), their own judges and many families engaged in banking, silver-working, medicine, and other trades. Towards the end of the 14th century, the populace being stirred up by a profligate preacher, there was a deplorable general assault on the Jews. This was the start of the decadence of the Jewish quarter until they were finally expelled in 1483. The quarter included what is now the district of Santa Cruz and that of San Bartolomé, two districts of Seville whose attractive streets, facades, and small plazas are an invitation to take a walk.

Barrio de Santa Cruz. Start the circuit by crossing the Callejón de la Judería at the back of the Patio de Banderas. After going through an iron gate, you reach Calle Vida, which forms a quiet corner and gives you a chance to rest. The Callejón del Agua follows the wall of the Gardens of the Alcazar, and you will immediately run into narrow streets full of legends and flavour that should be taken in leisurely.

In the Callejón del Agua, there is a plaque dedicated to the Marquis of La Vega-Inclán. At the beginning of this century, he remodelled Santa Cruz to its current urban layout while he filled the newly-created post of Regal Tourism Commissioner.

Blanco White

On Calle Pimienta, you run into Calle **Susona** on the left. Susona was a rich Jewess whose head was hung on a pike on this same street when she was executed for treason. Continue along Pimienta and, turning left on Calle Gloria, you reach the Plaza de Doña Elvira. From there, walk down a narrow street to reach the Plaza de la Alianza. You can carry on along Rodrigo Caro to evoke the memory of Blanco White, a distinguished Sevillian who, as the plaque on the facade states, dedicated his life to fight against intolerance. The same Calle **Jamerdana** will take you to the church of the Hospital de los Venerables (*below*), a jewel of Seville Baroque architecture that is well worth visiting •*84*.

The **Plaza de la Alianza** owes its name to a nineteenth-century tavern that was located there, and where the most liberal social gatherings in Seville were held. It used to be called Plaza del Pozo Seco.

The Comedy Playhouse was located in the **Plaza de Doña Elvira,** and plays by Lope de Rueda and other popular authors made their debut there. Now it is a placid place where you can see Mudejar ceilings and balconies full of flowers. One of the city's greatest painters, Amalio, had his studio there.

The **Hospital de los Venerables Sacerdotes,** a home for retired priests, is a 17th-century building founded for the purpose by the Canon Justino de Neve. It is built around a central patio in a unique fashion with steps going down and a circular fountain. The entire church is a veritable work of art. Its walls are covered with pictures by Lucas Valdés which allude to the priestly ministry, except those on the vault of the chancel and in the sacristy, which are by Juan de Valdés Leal. Various altarpieces by Juan de Oviedo and sculptures by Pedro Roldán and Martínez Montañés are an example of the magnificent artistic content of this place. Nowadays the building is managed by the Focus Foundation, a private nonprofit organization in the city that uses it primarily as a cultural centre.

From the **Plaza de los Venerables**, also called the Plaza de la Hostería del Laurel, you can lose yourself among the narrow streets of Lope de Rueda and Santa Teresa and, after 'refuelling' in the traditional wine cellar that is located there, run into the Convent of Las Teresas and the house of the universal Sevillian Bartolomé Esteban Murillo. Crossing Calle Mezquita, you reach the Plaza de Santa Cruz, with the *Cruz de la Cerrajería*, a real jewel of Seville smithery, in the centre.

The Carmelite **Convent of Santa Teresa**, founded in the 15th century by the saint from Ávila, has a main altarpiece in its church with outstanding sculptures by Juan de Mesa: an *Inmaculada* in a central niche and, at the top, a magnificent sculpted group of *Saint Joseph and Child*. In the sacristy, various objects and relics that belonged to the foundress are kept in a showcase. You can see the convent atrium or *compás* through the simple side door.

The **Plaza de Santa Cruz** was created when the old church by the same name, now on Calle Mateo Gago, was torn down. As can be read over the facade of the house located at the east end of the plaza, the remains of painter Murillo and other illustrious Sevillians are buried under the site of the former church. In the plaza, notice the facades of the houses, such as the one at the corner with Calle Santa Teresa, built in the twenties by the regionalist architect Juan Talavera as his own residence. On the other corner is the Conslate General of France.

Murillo Gardens. From the Plaza de Santa Cruz, go to the Catalina de Ribera Gardens, or Murillo Gardens. It is one of the Alcazar gardens that was separated by the wall of the palace when it was donated to the city by Queen Isabella II. The Queen had a beautiful fountain built over the wall and dedicated to the noble Sevillian lady Catalina de Ribera. It has two beautiful figures of Triton, half man, half fish, from an orphanage in the Plaza del Pumarejo that was demolished in the 19th century • *116*.

n the centre of the Murillo Gardens, you will find a large fountain, a monument to Christopher Columbus and the work of the regionalist Juan Talavera in 1921. The monument to Columbus was erected on the initiative of the journalist José Laguillo, who organized a public collection through his newspaper, *El Liberal*.

On the other side of Avenida Menéndez Pelayo, which surrounds the gardens, an old 18th-century cavalry barracks (*see front elevations below*) is the seat of the **Seville Provincial Council.** This 'Council of the councils of the Province of Seville' is elected every four years by a thousand aldermen that are the result of the local elections to govern the different municipalities. It is a splendid renovated building with a square floor plan formed by two perimetral bays around a large central patio.

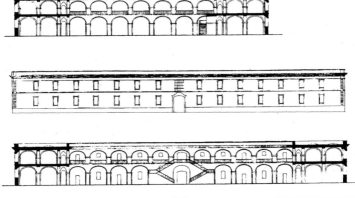

Puerta de la Carne. From the Murillo Gardens, carry on to the populous Puerta de la Carne or Meat Gate and go down Calle Santa María la Blanca towards the old Jewish quarter of Seville. The gate was sited at the confluence of Calle Cano y Cueto and Calle Santa María la Blanca and was demolished at the end of the 19th century. Named for the 13th-century Moorish architect who built it, Bab-el-Chuar, it took its present name from the city slaughterhouse that was built right beside it on top of, as the legend goes, the old Jewish cemetery. It was also called the Puerta de la Judería, gate of the Jewish quarter, since it was the only one that joined this neighbourhood with the outside. In the Archaeological Museum • *150*, you will see the plaques that were installed on it and the inscriptions about different historical occurrences. Unfortunately, it had to be torn down in 1864 as it had become a serious obstacle to progress because it did not allow large wagons to pass. Today, it is a place of continuous traffic with its own character and a noisy and motley crowd. It is a beautiful intersection that connects the intricate narrow streets of the old Jewish quarter with the wide, modern, rectilinear city, and with the bullfighting flavour of the neighbouring district of San Bernardo, a bullfighting quarter par excellence.

Santa María la Blanca. Go into the old Jewish quarter and, at Santa María la Blanca, you will reach its main synagogue, which has been the Christian church of Santa María since the 14th century. In the mid 17th century, it was refurbished, although the portal belongs to the first period. Its interior is surprising on account of the profuse plasterwork decoration, and the richness of its artistic content, such as a *Last Supper* by Bartolomé Esteban Murillo. The two half-moons under the cupola are copies of the famous original by Luis de Vargas, stolen by Napoleon's troops and now on display in the Prado Museum. You will notice the great frontal of the altar, work of the silversmith Antonio Méndez, and the cross and the candlesticks, which are made in an obvious rococo style.

A little further on from the parish church is one of the great palaces of Seville, **Altamira** (*above*), which is now being completely restored. The building has been enriched so many times since its construction (14th century) that its beauty has been compared with that of the Mudejar Alcazar of Peter I • *78*. Next, turn right to go into the maze of narrow streets; take a look at the dead-end street called Dos Hermanas, and then enter the quarter through Céspedes or Archeros—it makes no difference! First, Calles Verde and Alegría, and then you reach the Church of **San Bartolomé,** one of the few Neoclassial buildings in Seville, whose tower is outstanding. The building was constructed by Antonio de Figueroa (18th century) over one

of the four Jewish synagogues of the quarter. In its interior is the *Cristo de las Aguas*, to whom the Sevillian brides go so it won't rain the day of their wedding. Here you are in the heart of a popular area that demonstrates the survival of an urban layout with Arabic and medieval patterns.

Next to the Church of San Bartolomé, on a dead-end street, is the 17th-century palace where the poet Fernando Villalón lived (the one who dreamed of raising fighting bulls with green eyes) and, skirting the church, you reach Calle Levíes. There you will find the prominent facade of the **Miguel de Mañara Palace** (*below*). The founder of the Hospital of Charity • *128* lived there, as did the treasurer of King Peter, Samuel Leví, and the famous postmaster general, Rodrigo de Jerez (16th century). Today, it is the seat of the Directorate General for Cultural Heritage of the Regional Government of Andalusia.

You might like to finish your first itinerary of Seville with a good stopover to refuel at *La Carbonería* (Calle Levíes), curious establishment with a young, international atmosphere, and a very pleasant interior terrace located where an old charcoal warehouse used to be.

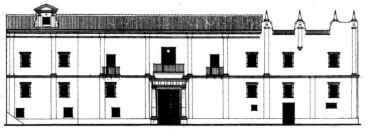

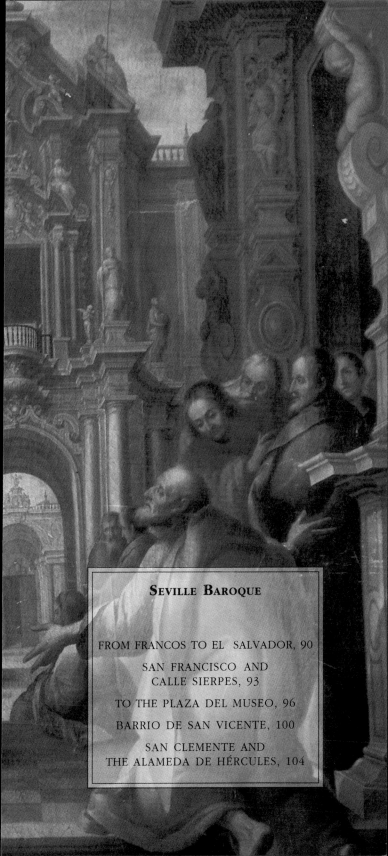

Seville Baroque

93. SEVILLA
Calle de O'Donnell.

This second itinerary will take you through the old city where you can feel the day-to-day life of Seville, see its central commercial streets, and visit the places you come across. The Basílica del Salvador, or Basilica of the Saviour, the central plazas and the City Hall, the Fine Arts Museum, and the San Vicente district, with its houses and palaces: a Baroque city with a native style that clearly shows what the *Seville Baroque* is.

"The Baroque was movement, a longing for novelty, love for the infinite and that which is not finite, for contrasts and for the bold mixture of all of the arts. It was as dramatic, exuberant, and theatrical as the Renaissance had been serene and restrained. The Renaissance aimed at reason: it intended, above all, to convince. The Baroque, on the other hand, appealed to the infinite, to the senses, and to fantasy: that is, it tended to fascinate."

On Alvarez Quintero. Start the walk at the Puerta del Perdón, which opens onto the Patio de los Naranjos at the Cathedral. Alvarez Quintero and Argote de Molina have a short stretch in common starting at the portals of Calle Alemanes. Take this street after having evoked the old wine cellar called Las Escobas (*left*). As a tile plaque above number 62 informs us, "Here drank geniuses such as Cervantes, Lord Byron, Lope de Vega, Dumas, Bécquer" Further along, at number 47, is the house of Ramón Carande, a distinguished historian and tireless traveller who is well-remembered and well-loved in Seville, and who died in 1986, just short of a hundred.

Calle Francos. Continue along Alvarez Quintero and turn to the right on Chapineros, skirting Peyré. Here you will see a group of regionalist buildings that house one of the most classical and elegant stores in the city. Before walking along Calle Francos, cross over to have a look at Calle Pajaritos as far as the house of the German Cromberger. Cromberger was the first printer in Seville and took the revolution of the printing press to the Americas in 1539. Go back to Calle Francos and stop to see its details and its old shops. There are old book shops (*above: San José bookshop*), lace and corset shops, furrieries, and shops with religious articles. Be sure to see the Reyes jewellery shop, a splendid example of Sevillian secular Baroque.

Plaza del Pan and El Salvador. Crossing the Cuesta del Rosario, you reach the Plaza del Pan, defined by the rear of the **Basílica del Salvador**, or Basilica of the Saviour, and a commercial building with a regionalist style designed in the twenties by Aníbal González. In this plaza, you can see the small shops that have embraced the side of the basilica since time immemorial. From there, besides, Alcaicería and Lineros streets begin and will take you into the midst of the popular and commercial hustle and bustle of Seville. You should, however, continue the itinerary, skirting El Salvador church on Calle Córdoba. There, you will be surprised by a tower that was a minaret of the main mosque of the city—Ibn Adabbas—where centuries later the church was built, Seville's second temple after the Cathedral. On Calle Córdoba, next to the tower, there is a gate that gives access to the **Placita de los Naranjos**, which is, as at the Cathedral, the ablution patio of the old mosque, although you can also observe structural elements from the Roman and Visigothic periods. In the patio is the small **Capilla del Cristo de los Desamparados**, or Chapel of the Christ of the Destitute, decorated with Baroque murals that offer indulgences for the masses that are heard there.

A visit inside. Also from the patio you reach the inside of the basilica through a corridor where a great stone tablet is displayed with a verse by the poet king of Seville, al-Mutamid, thanking the people in 1080 for a renovation that was carried out on the minaret at that time •23. The **Basílica del Salvador** was built in the 17th century. Its main altarpiece, by Cayetano Acosta, is one of the most representative works of the Seville Baroque. The vault that covers it was painted by Juan de Espinal. Acosta is also the author of the colossal altarpiece of the sacramental chapel, presided over by a splendid silver altar that shelters *Jesús de la Pasión*, the culminating work of Martínez Montañés. This temple holds several works of great value, such as the 13th-century *Virgen de las Aguas*, in the chapel of the same name, and the *Cristo del Amor*, by Juan de Mesa.

In this Basilica lie the remains of Don Carlos de Borbón and Doña Luisa Francisca de Orleans. This is where Princess Elena placed her wedding bouquet in honour of her great-grandparents.

The surrounding area. After leaving the basilica through its main façade, you will find the **Plaza del Salvador**, one of the most enchanting places in the centre of Seville. On the other side, beneath the porticos, are the crowded bars with good ham, good wine and olives. Next door, you can see the facade with Doric columns of the temple of the 16th-century **Hospital de San Juan de Dios**, which has an interesting 18th-century wall tiling on the inside. In the centre of the plaza, there is a bronze statue with an image of the sculptor Juan Martínez Montañés. To the right is La Alicantina, a traditional establishment specialized in the best seafood. To the left, over the wall of El Salvador, you can see the *Cristo de los Polaineros*, made of ceramic and which serves to remind us that it is the obligation of everyone, *kings, Moors, and Christians*, to venerate the Holy Sacrament when it is carried through the streets (dogma of Pope John I in 1387).

An aside. If you like, leave the circuit you are following for a few minutes and go down the busy and popular Calle Cuna until you reach the museum palace of the Countess of Lebrija (which can be visited some evenings during the week and which has excellent Roman pieces—superb mosaics and busts from Italica • 19). On the way back, you can go down Calle Acetres, which begins at Calle Cuna, to evoke at No. 6 the universal poet Luis Cernuda or, at the end, on Calle Buiza y Mensaque, the musician of all times Joaquín Turina. These artists were born and lived here in these houses. These are narrow streets where you can see how the *corrales de vecinos*, or collective houses, looked before being restored. Now, though, you should go back to El Salvador.

Sevilla - Plaza de la Constitucion

From the Plaza del Salvador, go toward the Plaza de San Francisco, taking a peek, as you go past, at the Entrecárceles wine cellar (*right*) declared of ethnological interest by the Regional Government of Andalusia. When you reach San Francisco, which always was and still is the main plaza of Seville, you will see to your right where Calle Sierpes begins, with the most rationalist café on the corner, the classical Bar Laredo • *33*.

Plaza de San Francisco. The magnificent plaza borders on the left with the Royal Audience Chambers, today the seat of a savings bank, and to the right with the City Hall, one of the culminating works of the Spanish Renaissance, and at the back, with the mammoth building of the Bank of Spain, built over the 'House of the Genoese', main banking house and centre of Italian commerce with the New World. The *Fountain of Mercury*, god of trade, still exists before the facade of the building. This sculpture was cast by the author of the Giraldillo, Bartolomé Morel. The fountain was not placed in the middle of the plaza because all types of Baroque pageants, bullfights, and even executions by the Inquisition were organized there.

The surroundings are completed by interesting buildings used for dwellings and shops. The historical seat of the Seville Press Association is located in one of them. The facade of the City Hall is carved in a rich Plateresque style by several artists of the period and, as can be observed, still isn't finished. Skirting the City Hall, you come to the Plaza Nueva through the little archway built over what used to be the entrance to the Convent of San Francisco, on whose land the main plaza of Seville was built. In the little archway, you can see the figures of Hercules and Julius Caesar, founders of Seville.

Legend of the souls. The chronicles of the Casa Grande de San Francisco convent (which stood on the Plaza Nueva until the last century), say that in 1600, the lay brother Juan Torres helped at a mass officiated by a Franciscan who had died a century before. The liturgy was celebrated in the Chapel of San Onofre, across from the right side of the equestrian statue that presides the plaza. With the help of the lay brother, the Franciscan was freed from the purgatory that he was suffering because he had omitted in life a Mass for the dead that had been entrusted to him. The chapel altarpiece, dedicated to San Onofre, is a splendid work by Martínez Montañés with paintings by Francisco Pacheco.

You reach the **City Hall**, designed by Diego de Riaño i the 16th century and built over the old fish markets, fron the Plaza Nueva. In its interior (visits, Tuesday and Thurs day afternoons), you are sure to be surprised by th *apeadero,* the stairway, the Mannerist Archive, and th Chapter Room (covered by a beautiful coffered ceilin with gilt panels, where you can see the 15th-century *bar ner of the city*), and also the vaults and cupolas.

The **Plaza Nueva** or **Plaza de San Fer nando** has a building with an interes ing regionalist style (offices of a tele phone company), and in the centr the equestrian statue of Saint Ferd nand, patron saint of the city. The mc nument was going to be built in hor our of Queen Isabella II, who paid for the plaza, but sh was against the idea, saying "I will have no statues whil I am alive." In this plaza stands the prestigious Hot Inglaterra, the oldest hotel in the city, dating back to 185

Seville Baroque

Calle Sierpes. This street is the central axis of traditional commerce in Seville and is thus called because it resembles a serpent in its course. It is a central point of the city where the movement of people is continuous. Full of life, it has lost today some of its traditional cafes that were replaced by the social circles that have their seat here and on the parallel street of Tetuán (such as the Athenaeum, which is worth visiting). The Royal Gaol was here (where a building was constructed that is now the seat of a bank).

In this gaol, Cervantes, for the astonishment and delight of all the world, conceived the Don Quixote while he was imprisoned under the accusation of having taken public money that he collected while he was a revenue officer.

Continue along Calle Sierpes. On this street, with Baroque balconies modified under an old decree to avoid indiscreet contemplations, the botanical garden of Doctor Nicolás Monardes was also located, as we are reminded by an artistic tile on the facade of a watchmaker's called El Cronómetro. This scientist, author of a *Natural History of the Things They Bring from Our West Indies That Serve as Medicine,* planted the first potatoes and tomatoes, the first tobacco and castor-oil plants, and the first caoutchouc tree that came to Europe from America. The curious clocks of the traditional watchmaker's remind us of the passage of more than four centuries...

On Calle Sierpes, there are traditional establishments, some of which have a marked architectural style, such as the modernist Ruiz jewellery shop, with a marble facade and a decorative grille. There are also shops with flashy ads, such as the wall tiling of Zulategui sports shop. At number 35, you can see what used to be one of the principal café chantants of the city, El Tronío, later called Café Madrid. Even today (changed into a hall for games of chance), it keeps the structure of the period. Hat shops, elegant textiles, and book shops compete with each other. There are two traditional confectioner´s shops known for their exquisite sweets: halfway down the street, Ochoa, and at the end, La Campana. **La Campana** is the commercial heart of the city with El Corte Inglés at the back.

After what used to be the Royal Gaol, on your left is Calle Jovellanos and the Franciscan **Chapel of Saint Joseph**, a sample of the Seville Baroque. It belonged to the carpenters' guild and is incorporated with St. John Lateran in Rome. The main altarpiece is by Cayetano de Acosta, with sculptures by Duque Cornejo.

36 — Sevilla. La Campana

From La Campana turn left into Calle Velázquez and then take Calle Rioja to **Plaza de la Magdalena,** where the parish church of the same name stood on the site of a mosque. Joseph Bonaparte ordered it to be torn down in 1811 to make way for a new square for the city. Several celebrated Sevillians, including Martínez Montañés, were laid to rest here. The fountain dates back to the 16th century and is the work of Genoese craftsmen. Continuing along Calle San Pablo, you reach the convent bearing the name of this saint, in whose church today's La Magdalena parish church is established. The Dominican Convent of San Pablo was the largest in the city and was founded by St. Ferdinand. It was here that Friar Bartolomé de las Casas, defender of the Indians, of the New World, was conse- crated bishop of Chiapas in 1525. The church is well worth a visit, as it conserves its medieval design and carvings by Pedro Roldán and Juan de Mesa, in addition to magnificent murals by Lucas Valdés and paintings by Zurbarán. The Sacristy houses one of the finest collections of gold and silverware in Seville. This temple is undoubtedly the second most important example of Sevillian Baroque after the El Salvador Basilica • _92_.

The Sevillian Friar Bartolomé de las Casas the son of a seafarer who took part in Christopher Columbus' discovery of America, is noted for his involvement in the fight against Indian slavery. He preached in the New World in the aboriginal tongues and, on one occasion, actually refused a sick man the Viaticum until he granted his Indian slaves their freedom.

Plaza del Museo. On the other side of the church devoted to Mary Magdalen is Hotel Colón, a sumptuous building constructed for the 1929 Iberoamerican Exposition. Traditionally a favourite with bull-

fighters and politicians, it is worth going in to take a look at the main stairway and lobby. Opposite the hotel is Calle Bailén, which takes you past the house where the poet Manuel Machado was born (corner of San Pedro Mártir) and on to **Plaza del Museo.** The square is shaded by huge magnolia trees, and in the centre there stands a monument to Murillo, the Sevillian painter. On one side of the square you can see the Baroque facade of the Fine Arts Museum, the former Merced Calzada convent. The building was renovated by Juan de Oviedo in 1602 and refurbished by Javier Feduchi in 1992.

Seville, the City

Visit to the Fine Arts Museum. As you enter the museum, you pass through a vestibule with beautiful 16th and 17th-century ceramic wall tiling. The building is arranged around three large patios, connected by a fine central domed stairway. Its atrium displays wall tiling by Pisano and Cristóbal de Augusta. It is the second richest art gallery in Spain after Madrid's El Prado Museum and is divided int fourteen chronologically arranged exhibition rooms. 15th-century exhibits includ a Virgin Mary by Lorenzo Mercadante and two striking groups of sculpture by h disciple Pedro Millán, including the *Burial of Christ*, a fine example of the chara teristic realism of late Gothic art.

In the **Renaissance Room** you will see Torrigiani's *St. Jerome*, an emblematic sculpture which influenced all Seville's subsequent plastic arts production. The most outstanding exhibits here are *The Final Judgment* by Maarten de Vos (whose nudes were proscribed by Pacheco in his famous *Arte de la Pintura*), *Crucifixion* by Lucas Cranach, and a portrait of Jorge Manuel Theotokópoulos by his father, El Greco. Further on, you can admire examples of early Sevillian Mannerism and Baroque aesthetics in works by Montañés, Pacheco and Roelas. In another room there is a series of statues of Child Jesus, of which the most notable is Pedro de Mena's *San Juanito*, and one of the most beautiful paintings of 16th and 17th-century Sevillian art, *The Last Supper* by Alonso Vázquez.

After crossing the **main cloister**, which features a Columbian relief by Antonio Susillo (a key figure in 19th-century Sevillian art) • _119_, you enter the **church of the old convent** which contains, amidst 18th-century frescos, the jewel of the museum: an extremely important series by Murillo, and works by Velázquez and Zurbarán _(The Apotheosis of St. Thomas Aquinas)_. The large _Immaculate Conception_ by Murillo is worthy of note, as is the set of works by this same Sevillian artist which formed the Capuchin altarpiece. A side chapel is reserved exclusively for the popular _Virgen de la Servilleta_, which reveals the mixture of piety and secular popularism which characterizes Murillo's work. You can now leave the church to enter the **Patio de los Bojes**, which features a Renaissance gate from Calahorra Castle and the renowned ceramic tile of the _Virgen del Populo_.

On the top floor there are rooms dedicated to the works of Valdés Leal, Ribera and Zurbarán, and a complete 15th-century coffered ceiling, the only remaining vestige of the palace of the Tavera family (demolished to build the department store El Corte Inglés. Finally, the rooms dedicated to Romanticism and Regionalism are particularly noteworthy, with interesting works by Antonio María Esquivel _(Girl with a Doll)_, Ignacio Zuloaga _(Ugarte the Painter)_, Gonzalo Bilbao _(The Cigar Girls)_, Gustavo Bacarisas _(Fiestas in Seville)_ and Daniel Vázquez Díaz _(Juan Centeno and his Cuadrilla)_.

Cristo de la Expiración. After the visit to the museum, make your way from Plaza del Museo towards the San Vicente *barrio* or district along the street bearing his name, which starts on the far side of the square. Before setting off, however, take a look at the original *Cristo de la Expiración*, a famous Mannerist image housed in the chapel attached to the museum building. It is said that the artist, Marcos de Capita, who completed the image in a fortnight, threw himself into the River Guadalquivir after the remains of the moulds of his masterpiece, having been ordered to hand them over to ensure that the Christ would remain a unique piece.

In the opposite corner of Plaza del Museo is Calle Monsalves, graced with magnificent mansions which captivate the visitor, such as the **Palacio de Monsalves,** well worth a visit just to view the excellent wall tiling of its majestic stairway and the interior patio. Opposite the palace there is a traditional little bar, with best quality *pata negra* cured *serrano* ham, and next to it, Calle Fernán Caballero. In the left half of this street, stop before the moument to the Sevillian writer Cecilia Böhl de Faber, alias Fernán Caballero, born to a German father in this house at the end of the 18th century.

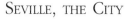

She led a troubled life of disenchantment, luxury and hardship. (She was spurned by Sevillian high society on marrying her third husband, a man much younger than herself, and this monument was financed, on her death, by the Duke and Duchess of Montpensier, two of the few friends she had left in the city.)

Barrio de San Vicente. Return now to Plaza del Museo to take Calle San Vicente, which will bring you into the district of the same name. This is part of the city centre, but also very much a traditional *barrio*. Treating you to both stately and popular settings, this route brings you first of all to the side of the refurbished **Palacio de Monsalud**

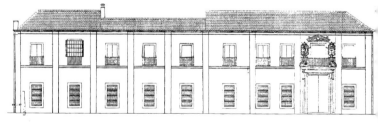

(elevation above), an 18th-century building whose main facade—displaying a stone doorway decorated with coats of arms—is to the right, on Calle Cardenal Cisneros. Opposite is the oldest Christian church in Seville, **San Vicente**, which was a Goth convent founded by St. Leander, and on whose walls an ancient plaque relates the story of the sudden death of Gundamaro, a Vandal king who was killed whilst attempting to plunder the convent. Inside, there are magnificent sculptures and important frescos by artists of the stature of Pedro Roldán or Herrera the Elder. The tortoiseshell cross of the *Cristo de las Peñas* in the Sacramental Chapel is of exceptional quality.

Following San Vicente Church along Calle Miguel Cid, on the left you will pass **Placita de Teresa Enríquez**, who was known as the 'Fool of the Sacrament' and was the founder of several Sevillian sisterhoods. Continuing along Calle Miguel Cid (a Sevillian poet who exalted the dogma of the Immaculate Conception), turn right into Calle Baños. At number 46 is the ***Cuartel del Carmen***, a building declared to be of cultural interest, and which was formerly a Discalced Carmelite convent (14th century). After having been an infantry barracks for over a century, it now houses the Music Conservatory and the School of Dramatic Art. Carry on down Calle Baños and, when you reach Plaza de la Gavidia, turn left into Calle Cardenal Spínola, where you will see, at number eight, the facade of **Santa Rosalía Convent**. This is

an 18th-century building whose church features an excellent Baroque altarpiece by Cayetano de Acosta and numerous paintings in tempera by Juan de Espinal.

At the end of Calle Cardenal Spínola you reach the Plaza de San Lorenzo, which was formerly the ablution patio of yet another Sevillian mosque on the site of which a Christian church was built, today the **San Lorenzo Parish Church**. This is a very Sevillian place where—as a ceramic tile on the facade of house number six informs you—the residents still miss Paco Palacios, *el Pali*, a genius of the *sevillana* • _37_, who died in 1988. Distinctive features glimpsed through the square's large trees are the Moorish minaret and the splendid ceramic tiling of *Jesús del Gran Poder,* which served as a model for later ceramic altarpieces. Inside the temple there is a magnificent main altarpiece by Montañés (with sculptures by the Dionisio de Rivas brothers). At the nartex side of the church, the chapel of the 14th-century *Virgen de Rocamador* (cited in Alfonso X the Wise's *Cantigas*) features interesting decorated wall tiling. Juan Ramírez Bustamante, who became the parish priest of this church after 65 years in the Navy, is buried here. At the time of his ordination he had 51 children.

Also in this square is the **Basílica del Gran Poder,** which contains the famous image of the *Señor de Sevilla* • _47_ (Juan de Mesa, 1620). It is one of the finest Sevillian Baroque images, in which extraordinary anatomical detail is combined with sensitive deep-rooted devotional values, greatly enhanced by the alteration of its original polychromy through aging. Devotees flock to the Basilica every Friday of the year to pay tribute to one the city's greatest treasures.

Before continuing on your way, you may like to tak a rest and recover your strength in Bodeguita San Lorenzo (corner of Calle Teodosio), which has been declared a centre of ethnological interest. It is a pleasant bar and a historic meeting place for locals.

Calle Santa Clara. Flank the ancient Mudejar tower of the San Lorenzo Parish Church into Calle Santa Clara—the main axis of the *barrio*—and you will come upon the palace of the Marquis of Torre de la Pressa (no. 12) and Santa Ana Convent. At no. 21-23 stands one of Seville's most beautiful houses, the **Bucarelli Palace** *(above)*, a building which conforms to the typological structure of 17th and 18th-century Sevillian *casas-palacios • 19*.

A little further on, you will cross the narrow street called **Hombre de Piedra** or Man of Stone and, looking to the right, you can see a stone torso at ground level on the facade of one of the houses. It seems that it is the remains of Roman thermae and subsequently Moorish baths, which were located there for centuries. However, it is also said that it is the body of Mateo *el Rubio*, a Sevillian who refused to kneel before the passing of the Viaticum.

Santa Clara Monastery. At Calle Santa Clara 40 stands the 16th-century monastery of the same name, declared a national heritage site, constructed over the palace of Infante Don Fadrique (the son of St. Ferdinand and uncle of King Sancho IV, who donated it to be used as a convent). Since the end of the 13th century it has seen uninterrupted enclosure by Franciscan nuns. The tower erected in 1252 during the palace period is preserved in perfect condition.

The convent is entered through a 17th-century portal which opens onto the beautiful atrium, sided by small buildings set around the orange tree courtyard. This is an attractive public area which is owned by the municipality, as is the tower. A Gothic portal, formerly part of the Maese Rodrigo university (16th century) leads from the atrium to an enclosed area with a pond, landscaped by Juan Talavera (1922), and in which the famous Romanesque-Gothic style **Don Fadrique Tower** stands *(above)*. Over the entrance there is a tablet with the following inscription in Latin: "This magnificently constructed tower was built by Don Fadrique. It is in itself the greatest tribute to art and the artist. This son of Hispania's King Ferdinand, champion of the Law, and of his wife Beatrice, was the favourite of his parents. If you wish to know or reminisce about those times, be told that this beautifully elegant, sumptuous tower was already in existence in 1290." Under its vaulted ceilings, the City Council exhibits interesting remains connected with the history of Seville.

The monastery is associated with the figure of Doña María Coronel, who later founded Santa Inés Monastery *• 113*, as it was here that she was pursued by a libidinous King Pedro and, in an attempt to preserve her chastity, decided, whilst running through the kitchens, to disfigure her face with boiling oil so as to dampen the monarch's unbridled lust.

The **entrance to the church** of Santa Clara Convent is to be found in the atrium under a Juan de Oviedo portico. Here an engraved stone marks the grave of a celebrated lady buried according to her wishes in this public place, as only the nuns (of whom six were daughters of hers) could be buried inside the church. The interior of this Mudejar-Gothic 15th-century church is a gem of the Baroque style and contains a high altar and four side altarpieces all designed by Martínez Montañés. The wall

ling (16th and 17th century) and the choir stalls and lectern 16th century) are other outstanding features.

The story behind the tower is of unrivalled beauty and passion. Don Fadrique, son of King Ferdinand, Conqueror of Seville, fell madly in love with his French step-mother, Juana de Ponthieu, the young widow of the deceased king. Don Fadrique constructed the tower for her in secret so that she could hunt doves without getting cold, but told the people that it was a watch-tower, an absurd argument which nobody believed, as the tower was situated within the city walls. Disapproval of their relationship forced the couple to part amidst tears, saying their final farewell, she from the royal boat on the River Guadalquivir, and he from the top of the tower.

San Clemente. At the end of Calle Santa Clara is this monastery, founded by King Alfonso X the Wise, although subsequently altered. Its atrium has been a place for social gatherings amongst locals, in which the painter Sorolla, the Alvarez Quintero brothers, Antoñita Moreno, etc. are still remembered. A 17th-century portico affords access to the interior of the church, one of Seville's most beautiful temples. A magnificent Mudejar coffered ceiling extends over the nave, whose walls are adorned with 18th-century frescos and excellent wall tiling attributed to Roque Hernández (16th c.). The main altarpiece was designed by Felipe de Rivas and polychromed by Valdés Leal, and an interesting work by the latter hangs in the Choir. Several works by his son, Lucas Valdés, may be admired on the side walls. Here is also the sepulchre of Queen María of Portugal, the wife of Alfonso XI and mother of Peter the Cruel • 10, who donated the most precious item of the convent's priceless collection of gold and silverware: a large silver gilt cup, a Gothic jewel of the 14th century.

Calle Calatrava. From San Clemente now head for what used to be the Puerta de la Barqueta, taking Calle Calatrava to Alameda de Hércules, the last stop on this second itinerary around Seville. Calle Calatrava, so called because King Ferdinand, the Conqueror, gave the military order of this name a large plot of land in the area to express his gratitude, is one of Seville's liveliest streets, where *Ideal Concert*, one of the first live singing cafes, was located. To the right is the small **Capilla del Rodeo** or Capilla del Carmen, a chapel named after the *Cruz del Rodeo*, a cross around which several of the Holy Week processions turned. It is said that the chapel was constructed by the Duke and Duchess of Medinaceli for the soul of their son, Pedrito de Ribera, who was killed there by the family of a baker girl of Calle Calatrava, after forcing his attentions upon her. This true story was subsequently fused in popular imagination with the myth of Don Juan Tenorio, with the addition to the famous work by Tirso de Molina of successive passages in which the character fell for a nun of Calle Calatrava.

Alameda de Hércules is one of Seville's earthiest areas, traditionally associated with the world of flamenco and bullfighting. Figures such as Joselito *el Gallo* or *Niña de los Peines* have some connection with this avenue, which was originally built on foul-smelling bogs in the 16th century. It was then that this area became one of Europe's most fashionable spots, where the aristocracy of the time strolled amidst springs which flowed from the *Fuente del Arzobispo* fountain. All that remains now of its past splendour are the columns lining the avenue, two of which were brought along narrow streets from their original location as part of the Roman temple in Calle Mármoles. The figures of the patrons Hercules and Julius Caesar on top of the columns are by the sculptor Diego Pesquera •*108*.

The crowds on Alameda de Hércules are swelled on Sunday mornings by a colourful and lively antique market and flea market •*56*.

Mudejar Seville

Calle Abades. Calle Abades is a side street o
the left-hand side of Calle Mateos Gago, which
is opposite the Giralda Tower. This is a na
row, winding street which practically bring
you to Plaza de la Alfalfa, and which is line
with mansions and houses from the last thre
centuries. The first stop is Pub Abades on th
right, an attractive establishment in a mansio
which is well worth a visit in the evening
Further on, you reach the **Casa de los Pinelos**
a mansion which is now the headquarters o
the Royal Academies of Fine Arts, Literatur
and Medicine. Your attention will be attracte
by its column-supported mirador and, inside
the two patios which incorporate Seville's di
ferent architectural styles: the grilles are Gothi
and the stuccowork Plateresque; the coffere
ceilings and the wall tiling are Mudejar. The house is one of the oldest in the city t
have been fully preserved since its construction in the 16th century. San Juan d
Ribera, a member of the House of Medinaceli, was born here • *110*.

Continuing along Calle Abades, veer to the right along **Calle Mármoles**, whic
owes its name to the large quantities of marble found in the area, as one of Seville'
great Roman temples was located here. You can still see three of the great column
of its facade, the other two having been moved to Alameda de Hércules in the 16t
century • *105*. Now retrace your footsteps and, crossing Calle Abades, take a bac
street called Calle Bamberg to turn into Calle Estrella, making sure to stop off at th
bar on the corner, Bar Estrella, an old *bodega* with *solera* wine, which serves u
succulent, original *tapas* (*cabracho* and asparagus patés, Sevillian *tortilla* or potat
omelette cake). On the right-hand side of this street you come to Calle Manuel Roja
Marcos, where you can see an old ceramic tile on the facade of the hospice whic
was called *La Gota de Leche*. Opposite stands the church of **San Alberto,** displayin
a beautiful Sevillian ceramic tile picture portraying St. Philip Neri. The 17th-centur
church and the tower are Baroque, and the latter has interesting decorative tilin
dating back to the 18th century. A Neoclassical altarpiece presides over the interior

San Isidoro. You now cross Calle San Isidor
and at the intersection with Luchana stands th
church bearing the name of this saint, a beaut
ful 14th-century building constructed on the sit
of a mosque dating back to the Caliphal period
The portal situated at the nartex side of the churc
is Mudejar, while that of the right nave date
back to the 14th century. Rising above the latte
is the Baroque tower, decorated with 18th-cen
tury ceramic tiles depicting St. Isidore and S
Leander. An excellent painting by Juan de Roela
The Passing of St. Isidore (17th century), may b
admired on the main altarpiece. Equally inter
esting is the vault of the main chapel, featurin
the figures of St. Ferdinand and St. Hermenegild
The majority of its chapels are of interest: th
Sacramental Chapel is decorated with lavis
stuccowork and has an excellent altarpiece, on
of the finest creations of the Sevillian Baroque
other chapels boast early 17th-century wall ti
ing, and in the temple there is a collection o
works by Lucas Valdés, Francisco Pacheco
Duque Cornejo, Pedro de Campaña and Ruiz Gijón.

St. Isidore of Seville, St. Leander's younger brother *(above)*, was born in 560 and at 18 was in charge of the Christian monastery of the city, which supported the Catholic St. Hermenegild against his father, the Arian Leovigild. He is the author of the famous *Etymologiae*, a master encyclopedia encompassing all fields of knowledge, without which it would be impossible to understand the thought of the Middle Ages. For a thousand years—until the Renaissance—it was the most widely used text book in schools and monasteries throughout Europe.

You then come to **Plaza de la Alfalfa**, a lively square which has always been a hub of trading activities: a Moorish *alcaicería* or silk merchants' district, a medieval marketplace, a Baroque meat market and, finally, esparto workshops, sharing the square today with bars and traditional bakeries. On Sunday mornings it is transformed into a popular pet market, specialising in birds, where you can purchase the finest singing canaries or the best trained hunting partridges.

From the Alfalfa take Calle Águilas, and you will be reminded of the Sevillian king as you cross Calle **Cabeza del Rey Don Pedro**. At number 16 of this street is the **Casa de las Águilas**, an 18th-century house with a magnificent marble portal with Corinthian pilasters and a balcony flanked by two eagles. A little further along, also on the right, you will see the facade of the **Santa María de Jesús Convent** (16th century) and the church portal, which features an interesting relief attributed to Juan de Oviedo. Inside there is a magnificent altarpiece by Pedro Roldán, also the sculptor of its images. In the side chapels there are sculptures by Roldán and his daughter *La Roldana*. A modern chapel of no artistic interest depicts St. Pancras, permanently accompanied by the parsley taken to him by people seeking work.

It is said that King Peter the Just, also known as the Cruel (14th c.), killed a nobleman during one of his escapades. He swore in public that he would display the head of the murderer at the scene of the crime, which he did, but it was a carved head and hidden from view. On the death of King Peter, the head was uncovered, revealing to all that the king himself had been the murderer. Legend also has it that when Peter was killed by his brother Henry, the latter ordered his head to be exhibited in a public place as a warning to his followers, the majority of Sevillians.

Calle Águilas leads to Plaza de Pilatos, where you will see the facade of the **Palacio de Medinaceli** or **Casa de Pilatos**, one of the finest examples of 16th-century Sevillian secular architecture. It was commissioned by the Governor of Andalusia, Don Pedro Enríquez, appointed by the Catholic Monarchs to curb the power of the Sevillian nobility. The son of Don Pedro Enríquez, Don Fadrique Enríquez de **Ribera**, Marquis of Tarifa,

travelled to Jerusalem in 1519 and, according to the inscription over the arch of the palace's main portal, made a land survey of the journey made by Jesus from the Praetorium—Pontius Pilate's house—to Golgotha. On his return, the marquis recreated the journey, using the same measurements, from this point to the Cruz del Campo (*above*), situated on today's Avenida de Luis Montoto. Since 1521, many of Seville's brotherhoods have gone in procession along the route marked by this illustrious traveller. The old Stations of the Cross start at a cross which has been on the facade of the palace since the 17th century • _46_, next to which there is a text

which explains that indulgences are earned by all those who pray before the Cruz del Campo on the Fridays of Lent. To the left of the cross is a ceramic tile which refers to the first Station of the Cross, which begins there. There is also a marble tablet on the facade which recalls that San Juan de Ribera, a member of the family who was canonised by Pope John XXIII in 1960, was brought up here. The bronze nails of the tablet bear the arms of the Ribera family.

Although the palace is lived in by the present members of the House of Medinaceli—one of the great houses of the Spanish nobility—it may be visited.

The visit. The palace's portal was designed in Genoa by Antonio María de Aprile in 1529. From here you enter the **main patio** which reveals lavish Mudejar decoration and magnificent wall tiling. The central fountain is crowned by a bust of Janus and statues of the goddesses Pallas and Ceres. The busts of 24 emperors are arranged around the gallery. On one side of the patio is the entrance to the **Praetorium Hall** with Mudejar style doors, a splendid coffered ceiling, beautifully decorated wall tiling, stuccowork, and Mudejar style doors. From here, you can go out into the Small Garden, where there is a pavilion with interesting plateresque window grilles. Then come the **Judges' Room** and the **Flagellation Chapel**, with ribbed vaults and, once again, interesting Mudejar wall tiling and

Mudejar Seville

stuccowork. The **Large Garden** was designed by Juan de Oviedo, and it is from here that the majestic stairway, below an exceptional dome, leads up to the top floor. Here you will come into the **Tower Room**, with a Pannemaker tapestry made in Antwerp and a *Pietà* by Sebastián del Piombo, both dating back to 1530. In the neighbouring rooms there are interesting paintings, such as a bullfighting scene by Goya, or a ceiling painted by Francisco de Pacheco depicting the apotheosis of Hercules. The dining room and the adjoining room also contain important paintings, as do the Archives and related rooms, which are hung with works by Lucas Jordán.

Calle San Esteban, off the square, brings you into the **San Esteban** district as far as the church, surrounded by mansions forming one of the largest precincts of the 16th century, today very much in vogue. Until recently its *corrales de vecinos*, or homes arranged around a common courtyard, have been the seedbed for the new districts of the capital.

In the middle of Plaza de Pilatos there is a statue of the universal painter of the Sevillian school, Zurbarán, which, during the 1929 Exposition, was located opposite the pavilion representing Extremadura, his birthplace. The paintings of the main altarpiece of the nearby San Esteban Church are by Zurbarán.

San Esteban Church, constructed, like so many others, on the site of an Almohad mosque, is one of the finest examples of the 14th-century Sevillian Mudejar-Gothic style. Dedicated to the first Christian martyr, St. Stephen, the building was sold at the end of the last century to be demolished. The timely intervention of the Sevillian Academy of Fine Arts prevented this from happening, and soon after it was declared a national heritage site and, in 1966, an artistic heritage site. At present it is in magnificent condition, thanks to the restoration carried out by Andalusia's regional government. The portals are early 15th century. The **main chapel** boasts a magnificent altarpiece made by Luis de Figueroa in 1629, with paintings by Zurbarán *(above: St. Peter)*. The frontal of the altar table is exquisitely decorated with 14th-century wall tiles, and the **Sacramental Chapel** wall tiling is in a class of its own owing to the form and Mudejar technique employed in its construction. The naves of the temple are covered by a magnificent Mudejar coffered ceiling.

The house at number 35 of Calle San Esteban has a niche on a level with the second floor on the facade giving onto Calle Mosqueta, which holds an old artillery shell in tribute to the cantonal state which was declared in Seville in 1873. The attempted revolution was thwarted by national troops who bombed this area of the city

relentlessly for nine days.

SEVILLE, THE CITY

Now backtrack to Casa de Pilatos and follow the side of the house along Calle Caballerizas which will take you to Plaza de **San Ildefonso**, where you will see the church named after this saint on your left. Two towers flank the entrance to this building, a fine example of late 18th-century Neoclassical architecture both inside and out. The main altarpiece has an allegoric figure of Faith watching over the Immaculate Conception. One of the side altarpieces is dominated by a mural of *Virgen del Coral*. A popular legend in Seville has it that the image is Visigothic, was painted in the 7th century

by a monk named Eustaquio, and was venerated even in Moorish times. Diverse sculptures by Pedro Roldán and Martínez Montañés are to be found in the chapels.

Opposite San Ildefonso Church is the entrance to the atrium of **San Leandro Convent**, a building which extends from Casa de Pilatos along Calle Caballerizas, to the Plaza de San Leandro. It is one of the city's earliest religious foundations and the building was constructed in the 14th century. At present, it is occupied by some twenty enclosed Augustine nuns, who are the makers of the famous San Leandro *yemas*, sweets made from eggs and sugar; a delicacy which may be purchased through the revolving window situated on the far side of the atrium •*31*, the entrance to which is opposite San Ildefonso Church. The entrance to the 16th-century church, attributed to Juan de Oviedo by the painter Pacheco, is a Mannerist portal in the **Plaza de San Leandro**. The square, shaded by a centenarian magnolia tree, is popularly known as **Pila del Pato** or the Duck's Basin because of the fountain which was moved here from Alameda de Hércules. On the corner, next to the convent, you can see an 18th-century mansion featuring a beautiful mirador with semi-

circular arches and, below, a portal with a balcony protected by a small projecting slate roof. Inside San Leandro Church, you will see a Baroque main altarpiece and several side altarpieces which feature works of undoubted interest, such as the relief of *St. John the Baptist* by Juan Martínez Montañés, or *St. Augustine* by Francisco de Rivas.

Plaza del Cristo de Burgos. Continue the itinerary along Calle Descalzos, opposite the church of San Leandro Convent, passing the traditional florist's *El Cautivo* on the left. This brings you to Plaza del Cristo de Burgos and, immediately to your left, you can see a 17th-century house with a facade with groovings and dormer windows and a beautiful mirador. The Romantic style square, also called Plaza de San Pedro, is filled with impressive rubber plants and steeped in history. This was Seville's first Jewish quarter and, later, the last Moors lived here, which is why it received the name of *Adarvedejo de los Moros*. When the Moors were expelled, a large house was constructed here, first used as a comedy playhouse, then as a house for fallen women and, finally, as Europe's first tobacco factory until it was moved in the 18th century to what is now the University •*144*. The College of Architects also has its headquarters in the square in a modern building which has won several awards.

On the other side of the square is **San Pedro Parish Church**, a 14th-century Mudejar-Gothic building with a tower, the lower section of which had its balconies removed after the Lisbon earthquake. The main altarpiece is the work of Felipe Rivas (1641), and the left nave houses the famous *Cristo de Burgos*, one of the oldest images of the Seville Holy Week processions by Bautista Vázquez the Elder (1573). At the nartex side of the church is the *Retablo de la Paz* altarpiece by Pedro Campaña. The altarpiece of the Sacramental Chapel boasts a *Nazarene* by Felipe de Rivas and paintings by Zurbarán and Lucas Valdés.

At the beginning of the street on the right-hand side of the church, stands **Santa Inés Monastery**, constructed during the second half of the 14th century. The Mudejar-Gothic building was built over houses donated for this purpose by its founder Doña María Coronel •*102*, who was the widow of Don Juan de la Cerda, *Alguacil Mayor* or Governor of Seville, and whose mummified body is displayed in a glass case in the Choir (together with the Baroque organ of 1700, later made famous by the poet Bécquer), embellished with paintings by Francisco Herrera (1630). The main altarpiece is presided over by *Santa Inés* by Francisco de Ocampo, and in the right nave another Neoclassical altarpiece displays a *San Blas* by Juan de Mesa (1617). The magnificent collection of gold and silverware kept in the convent includes an exceptional chest for the Maundy Thursday temporary altar, made from ebony and silver in the Mannerist style.

In the atrium of Santa Inés Convent there is a ceramic tile which evokes the memory of **Maese Pérez the Organist**, to whom Gustavo Adolfo Bécquer *(left)* refers in one of his *Leyendas*. The famous organist died while playing magnificently during midnight mass, and the melody could be heard at every Christmas mass thereafter, although nobody played it, until the instrument fell apart with age and had to be replaced by the present one, which dates back to 1700 *(above)*.

Seville, the City

From Santa Inés, continue along Calle Imagen until coming to the statue of **Sor Ángela de la Cruz**. In the street which begins here are the headquarters of the *Hermanas de la Cruz*, an order which was founded by this Sevillian nun, beatified in Seville by Pope John Paul II. It is in this house, where the poet Fernando Villalón was born, that she has been laid to rest. This order was so well loved in the city that during the Second Republic the very same revolutionary militia-men who were burning churches and convents escorted the nuns on their rounds. Then, as today, they went out in pairs to visit the poor, the sick and the dying.

Santa Catalina. Now retrace your foot-steps, turn into Calle Almirante Apodaca, the continuation of Calle Imagen past Plaza de San Pedro, and walk past the large house which was an inn called Posada del Lucero. You will then come to Santa Catalina Church, with its Almohad tower dating back to the year 900. It is a fine example of 14th-century Mudejar architecture, and its Gothic portal from the same period taken from Santa Lucía Church was installed in 1930, with the original Mudejar brick portal now contained within the vestibule. The main altar-piece is 17th century and the side chapels also have interesting Baroque altarpieces, such as the one in the **Sacramental Chapel**, a beautiful example of Sevillian Baroque, with paintings by Pedro de Campaña. Also worthy of note is the Chapel of Exaltation (with 18th-century wall tiling), presided over by a *Cristo* by Pedro Roldán. The angels and thieves of the altarpiece are the work of his daughter *La Roldana*. Outside, a beautiful altarpiece of *Cristo de la Exaltación* may be admired.

Turn right on leaving Santa Catalina Church, stopping to admire the details of Mudejar art on a side apse. To your left is **El Rinconcillo** (17th century), Seville's oldest tavern, which invites the passerby to take a well-earned rest. Of great eth-nological interest, the interior is an accumulation of history wit-nessed by coffered ceilings and old ceramic ads, and its tables are ready to offer those famous ome-lettes with the best *serrano* ham or the ever popular spinach and chickpea *tapas* into the small hours of the night • *32*.

You next come to the **Plaza de los Terceros** and are set to enter the busiest quarter of this planned itinerary. The square is a continuous hustle and bustle of locals, and **Los Terceros Convent**, a 17th-century building, which is now being used as municipal offices, has its entrance next to the church. The central patio is well worth a visit. The portal of the church has marked geometric forms, and the interior is dominated by a main altarpiece completed by Francisco de Rivas in 1669. The

Los Terceros Convent

stuccowork and murals which decorate the different chapels are of great artistic interest, as is the Choir, with its stalls and organ, dating back to around 1630.

Continue along Calle Sol until coming into the **Plaza de San Román**, the centre of one of present-day Seville's most popular *barrios*. Here stands the Mudejar-Gothic church dedicated to this saint, which is the headquarters of the *Hermandad de los Gitanos* or the Gipsy Brotherhood •*48*. The portal dates back to the 13th century, when the building was erected. The tower is from 1700 and has a bell section flanked by twisted columns. If you have time, you can go further along Calle Sol to number 130, the **Palacio del Rey Moro** or the Palace of the Moorish King, one of the city's oldest houses. Nearby is the *Corral de Valdecantos*, a very old house with homes arranged around a central patio.

From Plaza de San Román take Calle Enladrillada and then turn left to **Santa Paula Monastery**, Seville's largest monument. It comprises an array of buildings with a complex layout, which explains the density of the space it occupies, giving onto different streets and squares. The main entrance to the convent is through a beautiful 16th century portal which affords access to the monastery's delightful atrium. The entrance to the church, located here, is an extraordinary portal dating back to 1504, embellished with an exceptional ceramic tile picture by Niculoso Pisano and round mouldings by Pedro Millán. It is the city's most representative work from the period of the Catholic Monarchs and the earliest Renaissance ornamental piece to be found in Seville. A sculpture of St. Paula by Andrés de Ocampo presides over the main altarpiece of the church, and in the nave are the tiled sepulchres of the Marquis and Marquise of Montemayor, the founders of the monastery. The altarpiece of *St. John the Evangelist* is by Alonso Cano and the image that presides over it is by Martínez Montañés.

Sevilla. Portada de la iglesia del Convento de Santa Paula

Visit to the Santa Paula Museum. Leaving the atrium, you can enter the convent through a side door, ringing the doorbell for one of the resident Hieronymites to show you around the museum contained within the walls of its enclosure. The visit includes the old church, with a beautiful 17th century coffered ceiling, from which you can admire one of the enclosure's cloisters, the upper choir and a series of rooms displaying works of great artistic interest. A 16th century *Virgen de Guadalupe*, one of the rarest collections of Napolitan and Sevillian Child Jesuses in the world, an altarpiece by Alonso Cano, a *San Juanito* by Juan de Astorga, and a *St. Jerome* by El Bosco are just some of the works exhibited in the museum. Before leaving the monastery, you may wish to purchase some of the twenty-one varieties of jam made by the nuns, or madeleines which they also bake themselves.

Calle Santa Paula takes you to **Plaza de Santa Isabel**, where the convent of the same name stands, displaying a beau-

tiful bell gable. The entrance, which is next to the fountain, is a splendid portal with an Ocampo relief dating back to 1609. The convent was founded in 1490, although all that re-

mains from that period is one of its cloisters. Some of its altarpieces are 17th century masterpieces, such as the *Cristo de la Misericordia* altarpiece by three great artists of the time: Juan de Oviedo, Martínez Montañés and Juan de Mesa.

Leading off from Plaza de San Marcos is **Calle San Luis**, Macarena's main axis, also called *Camino Real* or Royal Highway, as this was the route the monarchs took when entering Seville. According to the inscription on a marble tablet in the vestibule, the impressive house at number 35 was a school for 'reading and writing'. Carry on until you come to **San Luis Church**, an example of Baroque exaltation second to none in the city. Built in the 18th cen-

Aquamanile

tury as a temple for Jesuit novices, it contains three altarpieces carved by Duque Cornejo and walls decorated with frescos by Lucas Valdés and Domingo Martínez. The temple is of Roman inspiration, with an awe-inspiring dome over the transept and balconies supported by great wreathed columns.

Santa Isabel Convent is next to **San Marcos Church**, whose facade gives onto the square of the same name. The church is 14th century and has a Mudejar tower. Opposite stands the house of Isabela, the *española inglesa*, or English Spanish girl, of Cervantes' *Novelas Ejemplares*. A special atmosphere reigns in this square, as it is a traditional meeting place for members of brotherhoods, sculptors, gold and silversmiths, painters and those who love the city.

A short distance from here on your right is **Santa Marina Church**, a Gothic building in spite of the tower's Mudejar decoration. The church was remodelled by Peter I at the beginning of the 14th century and the main portal dates from this time. The little square in front of the church is a place where meetings are held to discuss literature and theatre, as is **Plaza del Pumarejo**, which you pass on your right. It is here that the royal flour mill was located in the times of Charles III, according to an ancient tablet which is now exhibited in the municipal museum in the Tower of Don Fadrique • *102*. The square is an urban space dating back to the 18th century when the palace was constructed for Don Pedro Pumarejo, whose coat of arms is displayed on the facade. Although the interior is in disrepair, the columns of the patio made of ebony brought from India may still be observed.

Continue along Calle San Luis, with its traditional shops, bars and pubs crammed with bullfighting memorabilia and photographs of the Virgin Mary. These are places for *tertulias* attended by locals and a generous sprinkling of artists and poets. At the end of the street is **San Gil Church**, which dates back to the 13th century, although it has since

undergone several transformations, and where you can admire a beautiful aquamanile *(illustration page 116)*. The sanctuary and the transept, which was the original church's only nave, belong to the earliest period. The wall tiling of the presbytery is also 13th century. The tower is Mudejar, although the bell section was added in the 18thcentury.

You now come to the **Macarena Archway** and the **Almoravid Walls** which stretch from this gateway. They were built in the first half of the 12th century using lime and pebblestone and are up to two metres thick. They are defensive walls which surrounded the city until the mid 19th century. This is the best preserved section and extends to the right as far as the Puerta de Cordoba, which is attached to San Hermenegildo Church. Between the two gates there are seven towers which are solid barbican towers, except for **Torre Blanca**, which is hexagonal and has two floors with vaulted ceilings. In all there were seven kilometres of

N.º 9. - SEVILLA. Puerta de la Macarena

walls, 166 fortified towers, 12 major gates and 3 minor gates, including the Postigo del Aceite or Gate of Oil • *129*, the only one, along with the **Puerta de la Macarena,** that survives. The Macarena Gate is the result of a transformation that the gates of the city underwent in the 16th century: once they were no longer used for defence, they were widened to accommodate urban progress, which explains the monumental appearance of the gate. It is said that it was given the Greek name, Macarena, which was diffused to the Virgin and to the whole of the city, because it was dedicated by Julius Caesar to a daughter of Hercules of this name. Legend also has it that a Roman emperor murdered his eldest son and buried him under the arch to render the city invincible. The modern Macarena Basilica is also situated here.

Macarena Basilica. This is the seat of the most popular of Seville's brotherhoods • *48*, and houses—in an exquisitely worked silver alcove open to the public—the image of the city's best loved Virgin: Esperanza Macarena. This magnificent Baroque carving in the purest Sevillian School style is late 17th century and is the work of an unknown artist. The feminine expression of her face evokes an innermost feeling of hope, and her image represents the pinnacle of Sevillian Madonna iconography. The museum exhibits interesting pieces relating to her attire, such as the lamé and gold thread mantle embroidered in 1919 by Rodríguez Ojeda, a masterpiece of Sevillian embroidery • *50*.

It is said that the **Torre Blanca** was inhabited by the devil *Cascarrabia* transformed into the figure of a monkey and, later, the goblin *Navilargo*, who walked along the walls throwing stones at passersby. Later still, an old lady from the neighbourhood, Tía Tomasa, lived there.

SEVILLE, THE CITY

At this point, and before returning to the historic centre of the city through the exhilarating hustle and bustle of the route marked for the visitor by Calle Feria, why not take a break—next to the Macarena Basilica is a shop selling the typical *pescaíto frito* or fried fish, and opposite, a shop selling *churros*, deep-fried twists of

batter, which are among the best in the city—after which you can extend you itinerary to include two more interesting visits: the first to the Andalusian Parlia ment, set across a wooded area located opposite the famous archway, and the othe to San Fernando cemetery, a bus or taxi ride away, but well worth the effort.

The Andalusian Parliament is democratically elected every four years and legislates on issues as designated by the Statute of Autonomy for Andalusia. It is made up of 119 deputies belonging, in order of numerical importance, to *Partido Socialista, Partido Popular, Izquierda Unida, Partido Andalucista,* and *Partido Andaluz de Progreso.*

The Andalusian Parliamen

It occupies the magnificer building formerly the Hospit de las Cinco Llagas, which, fc many years, laid claim to bein the most important hospital i Europe, along with the Hospi tal Mayor of Milan (1456). was built in 1540 (to the de sign of the architects Martín d Gaínza and Hernán Ruiz) by th Ribera family, one of the nc blest families in Spain and th most important in Seville at tha time • *110*. It operated as hospital up until 1972, and was in its heyday, a source of inspi ration to hospitals being set u in Western Europe and Lati America. Access is gaine through a gate in front of th main facade of the building Inside, the church (today th Parliament's assembly hall), i one of the most outstandin works of Spanish Mannerism.

San Fernando Cemetery. Built in 1853, Seville's great necropolis is undoubtedly a reflection of the history of the city which encircles it. The architectural style, stark at the entrance and in the first pavilions, evolves in time with the participation of the city's most prominent architects. Noble and aristocratic at the start, it grows bourgeois and regionalist, finally becoming populous in the niche area. The cemetery is a haven of peace, its avenues lined with tall cyprus trees and geranium beds. In November it is an explosion of colour, ablaze with the flowers which the people of Seville traditionally place on the graves at this time of year. The yellow of the chrysanthemum becomes part of the cemetery.

On the left as you enter the cemetery are the graves of bullfighters and other famous people, including Joselito's grave by Benlliure, on which a group of gypsies cast in bronze contrasts with the white marble of the face of the bullfighter, whom they are carrying shoulder high *(above)*. There also lies Ignacio Sánchez Mejías, and in front of the mausoleum is the grave of Francisco Rivera *Paquirri*, with a statue of this bullfighter performing his last pass. In this area you can also see the graves of Juan Belmonte and *El Espartero* and, between them, those of the flamenco singers *Niña de los Peines* and *El Pinto*. The grave of the painter José Villegas is of a remarkable size, inspired by one of his most significant works, *The Triumph of the Dogaressa*. At the centre of the cemetery is the *Christ of Honey (right)*, the last work of the sculptor Antonio Susillo who, in response to public pressure on the Church, was buried at the foot of the statue after committing suicide for love in 1896. Also of interest is the small enclosure reserved for Muslims.

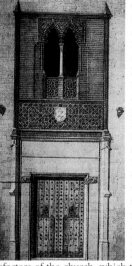

Calle Parras. To return to the Macarena district, and this time to the very heart of it, you pass under the archway or former gate. Then turn right into Calle Bécquer, take an immediate left into Bohórquez and continue along Escoberos until you come to **Calle Parras**, also on the left. This is the nerve centre of the *barrio,* a good example of the people's Seville steeped in tradition. This is the atmosphere which pervades the remainder of the itinerary, inexorably linked to the concept of a medieval town, which is still very much alive in all its facets. Worth special attention is Calle Parras 28, designed by Espiau in 1901, and today converted into the elegant Hotel San Gil. Number 13 is a popular tinsmith's workshop. You will now see how Calle Parras takes one along Relator to Amargura, and how the latter develops into a market, delineated by the apse of one of the Mudejar churches on the route. To the left you can admire the Mudejar polychrome balcony of the **Palace of the Marquis and Marquise of La Algaba**, *(above)*, benefactors of the church, which they used to enter, in days gone by, across a projecting walkway. This was demolished when, in the last century, it was ordered that all the city's archways and gates be destroyed. It is best to come here before 2 pm, as after this time the market is closed. In the **market**—the oldest in Seville (1719)—, all kinds of food and household goods are on sale, from buttons to snails and olives. And now you come out onto Calle Feria.

Sevilla. Mercado del Jueves

Although **Calle Feria** (which is fragmented into distinctive stretches) is associated with carpenters, wool dealers, sackcloth craftsmen, ragmen and other tradesmen—amongst whom Bartolomé Esteban Murillo carried out his apprenticeship—its essential identification is with the secondhand dealers who, for centuries, have sold their wares in the first stretch of the street, which you enter on leaving the market. In **El Jueves**, junk dealers and antique dealers come together to form a flea market which, from time immemorial, increases dramatically in size on Thursday mornings (hence the name) from 9 am to 2 pm, when the place buzzes with potential buyes haggling over the most singular objects • *56*. All kinds of bric-a-brac may be bought in this street, where some years ago an ordinary Sevillian, Juan de Mata Carriazo, discovered the Carambolo treasure, the oldest, most precious jewel in the western world and symbol of the city • *23*, *28* and *150*. It is also a place often frequented by *Rinconete and Cortadillo*, famous Miguel de Cervantes characters.

Next to Calle Feria's food market stands **Omnium Sanctorum Church**, a parish church since 1249. It is a fine example of Sevillian Mudejar-Gothic architecture, and has been reconstructed on several occasions, as in 1356 after being damaged in an earthquake, and

SEVILLA
OMNIUM SANTORUM

in 1936 after being burned down during the Civil War. It was here that the *Pendón Verde* uprising took place in protest against the high cost of living, and was mercilessly crushed by the *Cabildo* or City Council in 1521. The portal, carved in stone, belongs to its earliest period, while the tower was built in the early 14th century. The most outstanding feature of the latter is the *sebka* decorated facing inspired by the Giralda Tower. Inside, the chancel, although modern, contains the *Virgen de Todos los Santos* made by Roque Balduque in 1554. Also of interest is Ocampo's *Crucificado*, carved in the 16th century. The church is the seat of the *Hermandad de los Javieres*, a brotherhood which was founded by Jesuits.

69. SEVILLA.—El Jueves.

Calle Feria passes through **Plaza de Montesión**, which contains the chapel of the brotherhood of the same name. Next door is a quaint old bar, and further on—but still on Calle Feria—stands **San Juan de la Palma Church**, which has an elegant bell gable and which received its name from a palm tree growing outside. A subsequently remodelled Mudejar-Gothic construction, vestiges of its earliest period include the portal, the lower section of the tower and the vault of the Sacramental Chapel (with paintings by Lucas Valdés). The main Rococo style altarpiece features the image of *The Grieving Virgin Mary accompanied by St. John*, an exceptional 18th-century carving by Hita del Castillo. The sculpture *Cristo del Silencio* is attributed to Roldán.

"Esta luz de Sevilla... El palacio
donde nací con su rumor de fuente"

A. MACHADO

Opposite San Juan de la Palma Church is what remains of the **Casa de los Artistas** or the House of Artists, which was a palace in the 17th century, later occupied by painters' and sculptors' studios. It has now fallen into disrepair and is a storehouse for bric-a-brac and old relics. Following the side wall of San Juan de la Palma Church, you come to the **Palacio de las Dueñas,** the

residence of the House of Alba, Spain's most important family as regards the number of titles it holds. It is presently occupied by the Duchess of Alba and her family. The poet Antonio Machado was born here, and in its patios set down for posterity his childhood memories of Seville. The building as a whole, comprising the monument and the house, presents a short setoff facade with the coat of arms in ceramic (18th century) over the tympanum. It is not usually possible to visit the house, but inside here is a porticoed patio surrounded by gardens and decorated with beautiful stuccowork. The **Summer Dining Room** and the **Oratory** are unique creations in the city's palatial architecture.

And it is here that your itinerary comes to an end at **Plaza de la Encarnación**, which you will reach through Calle Regina at San Juan de la Palma. Along Calle Laraña, on the right, is La Campana; straight ahead, beyond the centenarian magnolia trees of Plaza de la Encarnación, Calle Puente y Pellón, the mainstay of Seville's traditional shopping areas, which will take you past time-honoured establishments and across Calle Lineros and Calle Córdoba to Plaza del Salvador and, just a few steps away, Plaza Nueva.

Seafaring Seville

This itinerary begins at **Puerta de Jerez**, where, up until the last century, one of the city's main gates stood. Today, it is still a gateway to Avenida de la Constitución and the historic city centre, and a through point to other areas of Seville. In the centre stands a fountain as a monument to the city, with a beautiful woman surrounded by joyful cherubs, built for the 1929 Iberoamerican Exposition. The plaza is surrounded by palaces and gardens. The **Santa María de Jesús Chapel** on the right marks the beginning of Avenida de la Constitución, and is what remains of the first University of Seville (which is reproduced on its main altarpiece in one of the most important works by the painter of German origin, resident in Seville, Alejo Fernández), built by Maese Rodrigo in 1506. The chapel is now the seat of the Council for all the brotherhoods and its most outstanding features, in addition to the altarpiece, include

The **Palacio de Yanduri** was constructed on the site of the demolished palace of the Lord of Cantillana, Juan Antonio Vicentelo de Lecca (16th century). The poet of the Generation of 27 and Nobel Prize winner, Vicente Aleixandre, was born here in 1898, as confirmed by the tablet affixed to the facade of the building now standing, which is occupied by a bank and which dates back to the beginning of this century. It was commissioned by Pedro Zubiría e Ibarra in the distinctive style of Madrilenian rationalism. The patio allows you to glimpse, through a beautiful gateway, the dividing wall of the gardens of the Alcazar. Above the lavishly decorated stairway is a splendid vault. Calle San Fernando begins at Puerta de Jerez by the Hotel Alfonso XIII, and will bring you to the next itinerary • _142_.

the wall tiling and the frontal of the altar in gold sheened ceramic.

The **María Cristina Gardens** (_below_) were designed in 1840 in honour of the Regent, the mother of Isabel II, on the site of the old Jardines del Abanico. Curiously enough, it was here that the monument by the sculptor Echegoyán to the President of the First Republic, Emilio Castelar, was erected during the Second Republic and respected by Franco's regime. Much loved in Seville, Castelar was responsible for abolishing slavery in the then Spanish colonies of Cuba and Puerto Rico. The Puerta de Jerez fountain is flanked by the **Palacio de Guardiola** on the left and the **Palacio de Yanduri** opposite. The first dates back to 1890 and is occupied by the Guardiola family. The portal is neo-Renaissance (be sure not to miss the patio decorated with lavish stuccowork). On the side wall (corner of Calle Maese Rodrigo and Puerta de Jerez), you can see the tablet which was originally affixed to the Puerta de Jerez in 1578, with the following inscription:

"Hércules me edificó / Julio César me cercó / de muros y torres altas / el Rey Santo me ganó / con Garci Pérez de Vargas."

Seafaring Seville

Continue on your way past the Palacio de Yanduri and take Calle San Gregorio to the beautiful **Plaza de la Contratación**. On the opposite side of the square stands the old Casa de la Contratación, or House of Trade, which today houses the Public Works Department of the regional government of Andalusia. You can go inside and see the central patio *(above)*, a fine example of Almohad architecture, the remains of which are carefully preserved. It is here that the earliest New World cartography work was drawn up, with the drafts by Amerigo Vespucci, Juan de la Cosa and the son of the discoverer, Hernando Columbus.

Leaving this public building, there is a cul-de-sac on the left, which leads to a beautiful spot called **Plaza de Mariana de Pineda**. Returning to Plaza de la Contratación you will see a Neoclassical building which houses the offices of the city's **Chamber of Commerce** (with an interesting interior patio in which the remains of part of the ancient city walls are preserved) and, opposite, Vitrubio Bookshop, specialised in the subject of architecture and boasting an elegant avant-garde design. Having passed the Chamber of Commerce, turn left into Calle Miguel de Mañara. You go past the pleasant Café Sevilla on your left and under the **Arquillo de Mañara**, an Islamic construction as evidenced by the horseshoe arch framed by an *alfiz* molding.

You then come out onto Avenida de la Constitución, where you might like to pause to admire the turret named **Torrecilla de Abdelaziz** on the facades to your right. Before crossing the avenue, you might also take the opportunity to have a good look at the beautiful Regionalist building located on the other side. It used to be the famous **Teatro Coliseo**, which came near to being demolished with the blessing of the authorities. However, it has since been declared a 'building of cultural interest'. Now cross over and just past the theatre on your left is the facade of what was the **Casa de la Moneda** or Royal Mint, a building complex dating from 1790. It is worth going in to observe the alleys which formed part of the factory. Leaving by the door opposite the one you came in through (Calle Habana), you come out into the open and onto Avenida Almirante Lobo, which takes you immediately to the right to **Paseo de Colón**. On this same facade the popular bar Iberia serves up an exquisite *tapa* of oxtail. On your right as you stand on Paseo de Colón (opposite the Tower of Gold • *126*), you can see the

Casa de la Moneda

Tower of Silver

modern building of La Previsión Española, designed in 1990 by the architect Rafael Moneo. Entering the building you can see remains of the city walls, and the **Tower of Silver,** an octagonal Islamic construction, enclosed by 18th-century buildings. Leaving Moneo's building you can see the famous **Tower of Gold,** right opposite. Crossing Paseo de Colón you get a wonderful view of Seville, with Triana on the far bank of the river Guadalquivir, and of the beautiful constructions on the avenue, such as the **Maestranza Theatre** and the **Bullring**.

"The hermetic mercury, the divine elixir, moonwort, calamine, and brass, were all being put aside by the disciples of Morienus, Raymond and Avicenna, as so many ships were arriving full of gold in the form of bars, vases, powder, stones, statues, jewels."

ALEJO CARPENTIER

The **Tower of Gold** was constructed for defence purposes in 1220 and its name comes from the outer facing of golden tiles which it originally possessed. A thick chain was stretched from the foot of the tower to the other side of the river, blocking off the entrance to the port of Seville. The tower now has three sections, the first of which is dodecagonal and dates from the Almohad period. It houses the **Naval Museum of Seville**, whose exhibits include numerous interesting old maps, etchings and marine charts, navigating instruments, pictures and other pieces relating to the times of the Discovery of America when Seville established itself as one of the most important ports in the world. On the outside of the walls of the tower you can still see small tiles indicating how high the water level rose during the floods caused by the swelling of the river.

The port extended along this bank of the river Guadalquivir as far as the Bridge of Triana, and it was here that the galleons of the Royal Fleet used to dock to unload their treasures. Today the quays provide a pleasant walkway where several companies hire out small boats or provide boat rides on the river Guadalquivir and interesting trips downstream • *12*. Midway between the

quays and Paseo de Colón runs Paseo Marqués del Contadero and, once again on Paseo de Colón, there are some excellent pavement terraces and kiosks (formerly stalls selling water), where you may wish to savour the view and take a break halfway through this itinerary. From here you can admire the opposite facade of Paseo de Colón, with the Maestranza Theatre, the Bullring and interesting Regionalist architecture.

Seville and the Opera. The **Maestranza Theatre**, built for the 1992 Universal Exposition as one of the finest opera houses in existence, owes its location in Seville to the city's close links with this art form.

Mozart's first two operas *(Don Giovanni* and *The Marriage of Figaro)* are set in Seville, which has honoured the composer with a bronze by Rolando Campos erected opposite the Theatre. Other famous works are also set in Seville, such as the only opera composed by the acclaimed composer Beethoven, *Fidelio; La Favorita*, by Donizetti; *The Force of Destiny* and *La Traviata* by Verdi; and *Alfonso and Estrella*, by Schubert. Or the popular *Barber of Seville*, by Rossini. Without forgetting, of course, Bizet's celebrated *Carmen*.

The Real Maestranza Bullring is a splendid building designed in 1761 by Vicente San Martín and restored at the beginning of this century by the Regionalist Aníbal González, who also designed the surrounding constructions which house the museum, the chapel (altarpiece by Pedro Roldán, before which bullfighters offer up their prayers prior to stepping out into the bullring) and the premises of the *Real Maestranza de Caballería*, with a beautiful library containing paintings in distemper by Hohenleiter. The bullring is owned by the *Real Maestranza de Caballería*, which is an institution created by the Sevillian nobility in the 16th century. The centre of the main facade, which

Carmen, the beautiful cigar girl from Seville, falls in love with Don José, a sergeant in the guard which polices the Tobacco Factory • *144*. The latter, seduced by Carmen, abandons his uniform and, against his will and convictions but consumed with passion, becomes a smuggler. Carmen then tires of Don José and falls in love with Escamillo, the bullfighter. Blind with rage, Don José kills her at the gates of the Real Maestranza Bullring, opposite which a statue of Carmen serves as a reminder of this tragic story.

gives onto Paseo de Colón, is marked by the Puerta del Príncipe or Prince's Gate, decorated with marble slabs and a 17th-century gate (designed by Roldán), taken from a convent which is no longer standing. The inside of the bullring (which is also open to the public other than during bullfights) is a great oval in which the upper tiers are covered by a majestic gallery of semicircular arches. Other outstanding features are a late 18th-century presidential box and a series of strikingly attractive corridors and passageways.

Arenal de Sevilla. You are now about to visit the area behind the Bullring and the Maestranza Theatre, which is the district known as Arenal de Sevilla. It is so called because it used to be a large expanse of sand, which extended practically from the centre of the city to the river. It was inhabited by troublemakers—Rinconete and Cortadillo, Guzmán de Alfarache—who were drawn by the fiery atmosphere which reigned in the old port of Seville. The construction of the Bullring redeemed the *barrio* and it became one of the city's most beautiful districts. To get there, cross the small Miguel de Mañara Gardens—a statue of him looks down on the area—which are located to the left of the new Maestranza Theatre, from which you should start your trip. You then come to Calle Temprado and the facade of the **Hospital de la Santa Caridad**.

Also known as **Hospital de San Jorge**, it displays all the splendour of Sevillian Baroque and contains many excellent works of art. It was an institution created in the 15th century to bury those who were executed and those who were drowned in the river. When in the 17th century the Sevillian noble Miguel de Mañara (repentant of the disorderly life he led) entered the brotherhood as its head, the institution gathered strength and the hospital and adjoining church were built. The hospital made use of the shipyard premises constructed in Seville by Alfonso X the Wise in 1252. In front is a beautiful patio with panels of 17th-century Dutch tiles and a splendid Baroque fountain with interesting figures.

It is said that many of the rose bushes growing in the Mañara Gardens come from the rose garden that the founder of the hospital tended there.

The church of the Hospital de la Caridad, the entrance to which is on Calle Temprado, has attractive ceramic tiles on its facade depicting its patron saints (St. George and St. James) and the three virtues (Faith, Hope and Charity). It is the home to one of the

Finis Gloriae Mundi *In Ictu Oculi*

city's most important art collections. It was all orchestrated by Mañara, the Benefactor, in accordance with a message which proclaimed that only by practising charity could a Christian gain eternal salvation. This formidable lesson is illustrated in works by Valdés Leal, Murillo, Roldán and Simón de Pineda. At the nartex side of the temple Valdés Leal left his famous *In Ictu Oculi*, showing how death comes to man in an instant, and how death triumphs over life, glory and worldly pleasures. And on the right hand wall is shown the *Finis Gloriae Mundi,* to remind us that it is man's behaviour which will tip the balance in favour of good or evil. On the wall of the chancel are several works by Murillo, portraying other biblical scenes relating to the mercy theme. The **main altarpiece** is an excellent work by Pedro Roldán, which represents the burial of Christ *(above)*. Another outstanding feature is the beautiful iron pulpit embellished with a sculpture by Roldán. There are paintings by Murillo on the side walls of the church and in the secondary chapels, which are also decorated with more works by Roldán and Simón de Pineda. Four major works by Murillo are missing from the church (and from Mañara's iconographic message), stolen by Napoleon in 1810 and now exhibited in foreign museums.

El postigo del Aceite. Near to the church of the hospital stand the **Atarazanas**, the former shipyards of Seville which produced the Spanish Navy's first steam ship, the *San Fernando,* launched on the river Guadalquivir in 1817. The building was also the seat of the *Maestranza de Artillería,* the military headquarters of the war with Portugal and the first apprenticeship school in the country. In more recent years it was used as military barracks and has now been closed down. However, there is an ambitious project to make it the most important Andalusian avant-garde art centre. Following the building round to the right along Calle Dos de Mayo (opposite there is a typical tavern which serves up delicious *papas picantes a la brava* or spicy potatoes), you come directly to the archway which is the **Postigo del Aceite**, formerly a gateway affording access to Seville • *117*. On its monumental facade you can see the only civic altarpiece in the city, set there during the reign of Philip II to commemorate the restoration of the gate. To the left is the beautiful *Pura y Limpia* Chapel in the middle of the street. Next to the Postigo del Aceite, the Regionalist architect Juan Talavera designed a triangular-plan market in the twenties, where *El Postigo,* an interesting craft centre or market, is now located. Leaving through the other door of the market, you come to the heart of the Arenal district, a place crammed with people and traditional businesses. A sandy river bank in times past, this district was also called *Sitio de Aneas* because of the abundance of bulrush growing here, which is used to make chairs. In Calle García de Vinuesa (where one of the branches of the river Guadalquivir used to pass), which leads to the cathedral on Avenida de la Constitución, there are charming old taverns where you can sample the ***pescaíto frito*** or fried fish bought from nearby fish shops • *33*.

SEVILLE, THE CITY

And as you continue through the Arenal, you will come to Calle Adriano, behind the bullring, where the **Baratillo** (former name of the district) religious brotherhood's chapel is located. Going along Adriano, you will come, once again, to the Paseo de Colón. After crossing the avenue, you will come to the **Antonio Mairena Gardens**, next to the Isabella II Bridge. There, a bronze bust of the famous flamenco singer is set on a white stone pedestal in the shape of an

anvil. And the truth is that the voice of Antonio Mairena was unrivalled when it came to singing the *martinete*, the Andalusian flamenco song that originated in the gypsy forges, singing to the beat of hammer hitting anvil. From there, it is just a short walk to the *Muelle de la Sal* wharf, with its **Monument to Tolerance**, work of the sculptor Chillida and financed in part by the Sefarad Hebrew Association. From this point, you will have a magnificent view of the famous Triana Bridge.

Triana Bridge, which is in the process of being officially declared a work of 'cultural heritage', was built over what was originally a pontoon bridge—that is, a file of anchored boats which supported a rather unstable deck—set up in 1170 by Emir Abu Yacub Yusuf. The present-day bridge, which takes the name Isabella II, was built in 1852 and owes its design to engineers Steinacher and Bernadet who took inspiration for the bridge from the Carrousel Bridge in Paris, which no longer exists. The large iron rings, which lend the bridge its airiness, came out of the workshop of Narciso Bonaplata. Still on the Seville side of the bridge, you can see a small castle next to it, called the Castillete de la Caridad, which was designed by Aníbal González for the 1929 Iberoamerican Exposition. Behind the castle is another interesting work of architecture, the former *Almacén Real de Maderas de Segura* which was for many years used as a bus terminal. Across the street, there is a metallic structure by **Gustave Eiffel,** now one of the City Council's public information centres. And finally, after crossing the bridge, you are in Triana, the seafaring district of centuries past, and now one of the most famous and popular parts of Seville.

At the end of the bridge there is a small chapel called the Capilla del Carmen, by Aníbal González, with figures on its dome representing the Giralda and Saints Justa and Rufina, patronesses of the city. Behind are the remains of the Castle of St. George, headquarters of the Inquisition, and much later, site for many years of the popular Triana marketplace, unfortunately no longer open. But now it is time to go over to the Altozano, the gateway to Triana. Take a good look at its facades before turning left for a stroll down **Calle Betis** on the bank of the Guadalquivir River. You might want to take a short rest beforehand and get some of your energy back by having some of the delicious fried fish served at the **Kiosko de las Flores.** From there, you can see the statue of Triana's Juan Belmonte, one of the greatest bullfighters of all time. Another popular *matador*, Guerrita, said of Belmonte, "If you want to see him, don't wait to do it", thereby insinuating that Belmonte would soon meet his death in the ring. However, Belmonte didn't die until 1960, and then by committing suicide, some say, for love.

Casa de las Columnas

As you take a most pleasurable walk beside the river down Calle Betis, at number 59 you will come to a typical tenement house arranged around a central courtyard, the *Corral de Vecinos de la Inquisición,* which was also a splendid palace during the 18th century. Turning right at Calle Troya, you will encounter a ceramic-tile plaque, as a reminder that this was once the Monipodio patio cited by Cervantes in his *Rinconete y Cortadillo* where beggars and vagabonds once gathered. On the right is Calle Pureza, which you will take to get to the famous **Placita de Santa Ana**. There, a church built by Alfonso X the Wise in the late 13th century takes the name of Triana's patroness, St. Anne. This Cistercian-Gothic church—though with a Mudejar appearance—underwent thorough remodelling after the Lisbon earthquake in 1755. Its main altarpiece stands out as the best to be found anywhere in Seville. The religious imagery is the work of Nicolás Jurate and the 16th-century paintings are by Pedro de Campaña. Other works of art are the *Virgen de la Antigua* (1510) in the central nave and the altarpiece with the *Virgen de la Rosa* by Alejo Fernández (16th century) in the retrochoir.

On the corner, opposite the right side of Santa Ana Church and Calle Pureza, a typical Triana-style tavern offers you a complete list of appetizing *tapas*, such as *boquerones en adobo* or marinated and battered anchovies. As you continue along **Calle Pureza,** you will be entering the real heart of Triana. Here was where the Inquisition's 'wolves in sheep's clothing' lived, but it is also here where the famous Loly pastry factory has been for years. These traditional Sevillian sweets are something well worth trying, if just to bring back memories of the 50's.

Behind Santa Ana Church (Calle Pureza 79), is the **Casa de las Columnas**, an 18th-century Neoclassical building now occupied by municipal offices *(elevation page 131 and above)* and whose patio and imperial staircase make it worth your visit. And, as you go along Calle Pureza, you can take in more old facades, as well as see the typical wine-cellar taverns and wonderful signs painted on Triana-style ceramic tiles. About halfway down the street, you will find the **Capilla de los Marineros** or Sailors' Chapel which holds the popular Baroque image of Triana's Our Lady of Hope or **Esperanza de Triana** as she is known to the locals. She is Seville's *other* Virgin (the districts of Macarena and Triana each have their 'own' Esperanza, thus affectionately dividing up Seville's fervorous devotion to the Virgin Mary). This chapel is home to an age-old religious brotherhood founded in 1596. The 18th-century temple, however, has also been used down the years as a Protestant church, an auditorium for variety shows, a cinema, a warehouse and a coal merchant's. At Calle Pureza 60 there is a traditional *casa de vecinos* being called 'the Quema house'.

Patios de vecinos. Calle Pureza takes you back to the Altozano, which you will have to cross in order to reach the other side of Triana by taking **Calle San Jorge.** It is here where you will find the first workshops where the famous Triana pottery and tiles are made. There are others on streets to the left, such as Antillano Campos and Alfarería. The latter is parallel to Calle Castilla and both of them are worth a visit, if just to observe the spectacular patios overflowing with flower beds and hanging flowing pots. Some examples: in Calle Alfarería, no. 32 *(Cerca Hermosa)*, no. 119 *(El Naranjero)* and no. 138 *(El Corral de los Corchos)*; in Calle Castilla, no. 7 (where the television series *Juncal* was filmed), no. 16 *(Corral de las Flores)* no. 58 *(Corral de los Fideos)*, no. 88 *(Corral de la*

Sevilla.(Triana) Una fabrica de Cerámica en calle San Jorge.

Rana), no. 105 *(Corral de la Polvorilla),* no. 143 *(Colegio del Punto),* no. 158 *(La Casa Alta),* and no. 162 *(Corral del Romo).* At the beginning of **Calle Castilla,** on the right, is the **Callejón de la Inquisición,** which leads to the Paseo de Nuestra Señora de la O, on the bank of the Guadalquivir. And, halfway down Calle Castilla, on the right-hand side, is the 17th-century chapel of the brotherhood of **Nuestra Señora de la O,** with its bell tower decorated with Triana tiles. Along with its image of the Virgin Mary, you can see the famous *Jesús Nazareno* with a tortoiseshell cross, carved by Pedro Roldán, also author of the exceptional *Sacred Family* group of figures.

El Cachorro de Triana. At the end of Calle Castilla, you will have to cross a modern avenue in order to reach the **Capilla del Patrocinio,** where local residents proudly venerate their image of the *Cristo del Cachorro,* a masterpiece of Seville's Baroque art, carved by Francisco Antonio de Gijón in 1682. The powerful facial expression, the tenseness of the body and the sense of movement of the clothes are all the result of the artist's capturing the instant in which, as legend goes, a gypsy from Triana nicknamed *El Cachorro* (meaning 'Pup') died of a stab wound. This priceless figure came close to being lost when a fire broke out in the chapel in 1973.

And it is from here that you will be able to commence the last part of this itinerary. After crossing—at the lights—the major road coming into the city from Huelva and Extremadura, the SE-30, you enter the Isla de la Cartuja. Here, the ancient Santa María de las Cuevas Monastery gives way to Seville's avantgarde architecture created for the 20th-century's last Universal Exposition. Today, this ultra-modern area includes the Discoveries Theme Park as well as the city's Technology Park. Both of these, leisure and the future, reflect the two most visible legacies which Seville inherited from the historical event held in 1992.

Entering La Cartuja from Triana or by crossing the Cachorro Bridge (with a peculiar canopy, clearly a modern allusion to Seville's age-old custom of putting up awnings on streets against the bright sunshine), you will see the imposing **Torre Triana** to your left, a building designed by Sainz de Oiza as the administrative headquarters of the regional government. Next to it, the ultra-modern iron-and-glass **World Trade Center**, run by a worldwide business organization which manages the world's most impressive smart buildings, such as the famous Twin Towers in New York. And next door, the attractive **International Press Centre**, covered with white marble and reflective window panes, offering media staff the latest techniques in communication. This is the first step into the Technology Park inherited from the Universal Exposition. The Hotel Príncipe de Asturias is also located on the Island.

Access to La Cartuja. To gain access to the Santa María de las Cuevas Monastery, you need not enter the Discoveries Theme Park, although there is another direct passageway to the monastery from inside the park. The latter choice is advisable when entering the premises on foot via the Barqueta Gate (1) or Cartuja Gate (2), both located on Calle Torneo in the city centre, or when you are leaving your car at the large car park on the other side of La Cartuja. However, Triana Gate (3) gives you the opportunity to first enter the monastery area, with the park to the left, until reaching the ultra-modern World Trade Center building, using the nearby entranceway, next to what was the **Pavilion of the 15th Century** during Expo '92. Today, the building is used as a small convention centre, with interesting frescos by Guillermo Pérez Villalta and a beautiful re-creation of carrousel clocks. Here, visitors to the Universal Exposition were offered a view of the 15th century—when Europe shook off its medieval lethargy in a few short years to take on the shining splendour of the Renaissance.

La Cartuja. Construction of the Carthusian monastery began in 1418 on the grounds of the **Santa María de las Cuevas** hermitage, in existence for a century prior to that. The monastery was built

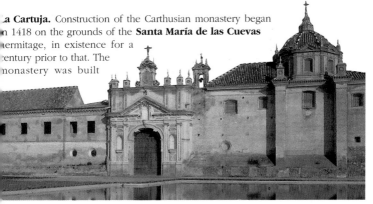

under the patronage of the Afán de Ribera family, one of the most illustrious in Seville's history • *110*. In 1519, the remains of Christopher Columbus were placed in the monastery's Santa Ana Chapel, in compliance with the wishes of the admiral who, during his lifetime, lived at the monastery and received support and encouragement for his voyage of discovery from the Carthusians. (His remains were exhumed, so it seems, some 18 years later and sent to Santo Domingo. They were brought back though, and are now said to lie in Seville's cathedral) • *69*. The Lisbon earthquake caused serious damage to the building and in 1810 it was converted by Napoleon into his southern military headquarters. Mendizábal's disentailment marked the end of its monastic era. Soon afterwards La Cartuja was rented by an industrialist from Liverpool named Charles Pickman, who installed a ceramic factory here. After being declared a national heritage site in 1964, it was expropriated seven years later by the Ministry of Public Works. The grounds were transferred to the regional government in 1982 and complete refurbishment of the premises took place. During the Universal Exposition, the monastery served as the Royal Pavilion, thus receiving visits from almost a hundred heads of State from all over the world.

At present, the lay-brothers' enclosure houses the **Andalusian Institute for the Historical Heritage** and, in the procurator's area, the Expo archives, comprising millions of images and documents from the event.

LA CARTUJA MONASTERY

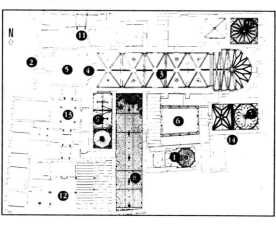

1. Santa María Magdalena Chapel, the former church. 2. Las Cadenas portal. 3. Church. 4. Ma[] portal of the church. 5. Atrium. 6. Cloister. 7. Chapter Chapel. 8. Refectory. 9. Santa Ana Chape[] Christopher Columbus' tomb. 10. Sacristy. 11. Access to Prior's cell. 12. Kitchens. 13. The Pickman[] residence. 14. Clock tower.

The visit. The visitor reception centre is located next to the Pavilion of the 15t[]

Century. From there, by following a path lined with acacias an[] jacarandas, you reach the Patio del Ave Maria, next to the mai[] facade of the Santa María de las Cuevas Monastery. From here you will visit the former church (1), the cloister (6), the refec[] tory (8) and two chapels (7 and 9). The temple's entranceway [] crowned by a large rose window surrounded by rhomboida[] ceramic tiles. The inside of the building is overflowing wit[] highly artistic wall tiling and breathtaking details such as th[] carved ceiling with lacery and pineapples covering the refec[] tory. Watch out for the frescos in the Santa María Magdalen[] Chapel (1) and the noble families' coats of arms in the Chapte[] Chapel (7). The cloister (6), although small, is an architectura[] jewel that transmits Carthusian peace and tranquillity.

The Chapter Chapel—the only sanctified place remaining in the complex, apart from the María Magdalena Chapel—has held the remains of the monastery's founders for centuries. Their present-day descendants, the Duke and Duchess of Medinaceli, agreed to have them returned here (after some time at the old university chapel on Calle Laraña) in exchange for a yearly Mass to be held on the festivity of San Juan de Ribera, a member of the family •*110.*

Once you leave this first architectural complex, you will undoubt[] edly better understand the reforms carried out by the Carthusian[] to enlarge it in the mid 18th century. A new surrounding wall wa[] built, along with a new chapel (with excellent wall tiling), and the[] monumental entrance and portal which today lead out to the[] theme park. Around the complex, you will enjoy a stroll through the outer gardens, the olive grove, the garden of Paradise and the orchard. The manufacturing area reveals how, for years, in Seville the best ceramic pottery was made here, under the name of Pickman.

The Discoveries Park. When entering the park through Triana Gate, you will immediately come to one of the most interesting pavilions remaining from the Universal Exposition: the **Pavilion of Navigation.** This magnificent structure, located next to the Indies Wharf, allows visitors to sail the oceans of its interior while being transported through the history of navigation. The visit includes a walk through the hold of a galleon and a moving walkway takes us through the Port of Seville at the height of its splendour during the age of discovery. The pavilion also offers excellent images of man and his relation to the sea. And suddenly, the entire building becomes a steamboat where you can take a rest on one of its deck chairs. An absolute must. Opposite the Pavilion of Navigation is the Pavilion of Discoveries which was never actually opened due to a fire that broke out shortly before the Expo. Fortunately, the **Omnimax Space Theatre** escaped the flames. The **Garden of the Americas,** a delightful botanical garden with samples of plant species from every American country that participated in the Expo, is located on the bank of the river. And to its right, the magnificent Auditorium, an enormous open-air facility adaptable to the needs of any type of performance and with seating capacity for some 5,500 people.

The company PARTECSA managed Seville's theme park on a provisional basis from 1993 to 1994, taking advantage of some of the attractions inherited from the Seville Univer-

sal Exposition. More than five million people visited the Discoveries Park during this first phase, which showed the world for the first time in history how the grounds of a Universal Exposition (in this case, the last to be held in this century) could be re-utilized.

And now, after having been awarded the contract in an international tender for managing the park, PARTECSA has put the complete renovation of the site into full swing. June 1996 will mark the opening date of the completely redesigned park with a whole range of totally new attractions. Some 11,000 million pesetas have been invested in order to carry out this wholesale transformation of the park, which will place it in the exclusive group of the ten best theme parks in the world.

This ambitious project will not only turn the Park into a unique tourist attraction in itself, making it a specific destination in its own right, but will also be another good reason for making Seville a place to visit.

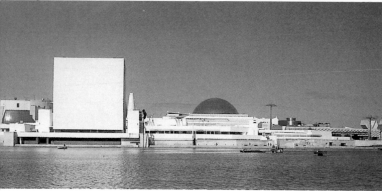

*In the picture above, the **Lake of Spain**, with the **Pavilion of Spain** overlooking it, where you can still enjoy the **Movimax Cinema**.*

As from June 1996, visitors will be able to enjoy the completely renovated premises, where education and entertainment combine to stage a non-stop fiesta. The Park will offer the best in family adventure with all kinds of fun and entertainment to be enjoyed by visitors of all ages.

State-of-the-Art Technology: The fifteen surviving pavilions of Spain's autonomous regions, which form an arc around the lake, will exhibit fifth-generation attractions, the ultimate in leisure technology. Due to the fact that the pavilions to be reutilized were so varied in appearance during the Expo, a multi-coloured metallic structure has been built to give them a more similar exterior appearance.

Night-Life Area: The area around the Barqueta Bridge and the Expo Cinema is an updated version of what was Expo-Night for Seville's renowned *movida* or night life. Its entrance will be separate from the Theme Park, with free access and open until very late.

Children's City: A wide range of children's attractions will be located north of the night life area, behind the regional pavilions.

The Ocean Blue: On the Lake of Spain, in the heart of the park. The aim is to provide a scale-model vision of the Old and New Worlds throughout the park; the lake thus becomes the Atlantic Ocean and the ports on each side of it represent the Ports of Seville and Cartagena de Indias.

Pirate Island: A man-made island has been built which will serve as a grandstand for watching the different water sports and shows which will take place on the lake. Spectators on the island, which covers nearly one hectare, will see the reenactment of a battle waged between a life-sized Spanish galleon, the *San José,* and a pirate ship, with actors performing in day-time and night-time shows.

Seaport: The lake shore area located in front of the regional pavilions, including the steps where spectators accommodate themselves to watch the nightly multi-media show, will become the port of Cartagena de Indias.

Port of the Indies: The canal has been turned into a Port of the Indies, maintaining the same type of scenario as the lake's, setting it apart from the rest of the Park. The banks of the canal will recreate Seville when it was known as the Gateway to America.

The Theme Pavilion: This will be the Pavilion of the Future, with a digital planetarium and activities relating to planet Earth using state-of-the-art technology. Both this and the other pavilions have replaced the walk-through system by one using mini-trains and aerial trams, which will allow for 1,500 visitors an hour instead of the 300 visitor-per-hour capacity for pedestrians.

Garden Festival: An imaginary line stretching from the viewing tower to the Guadalquivir River will divide the park's gardens into two areas. The northern part, nearest the lake, will have a more festive atmosphere. While still respecting the surrounding vegetation, there will be a number of attractions to liven things up, such as sailing down rapids in boats…

Mountain Peaks Area: In the gardens stretching from the viewing tower to the end of the Pavilion of the Future, a number of Sierra Nevada type attractions have been installed such as ski-lifts, bobsleighs, etc.

Mountain Village: An area with rides and other attractions for children is located in the area behind the auditorium and its hill.

The most spectacular attraction of the park is an aquarium worth more than two thousand million pesetas. Suffice it to say that there are only two other aquariums in the world such as the one installed in Seville's theme park.

The fiesta will be rounded off by lively street entertainment, a large selection of restaurants and a special programme of concerts, performances and film premieres for Spain. All of this with the expertise offered by its major shareholder, the American firm of Ogden.

Andalusian 'Costumbrismo'

The next itinerary also starts from the Puerta de Jerez. However, this time you will be going in the opposite direction, towards the South, following the course of the Guadalquivir River on your right. Behind the Palacio de San Telmo and the University • *144* the monuments built for Seville's 1929 Iberoamerican Exposition come into view. And one of Europe's most beautiful gardens, María Luisa Park, will take you inside the romantic Seville, that part of the city which has always characterized the spirit of this Southern European capital city.

Calle San Fernando, between the Puerta de Jerez and the Plaza de Don Juan de Austria, is one of Seville's loveliest streets. Named after the saintly king and conqueror, the street's origins can be traced to a stream which flowed here, the Tagarete *(above)*, a branch of the Guadalquivir which served as one of the city's natural limits.

The street owes its present-day appearance to the 1929 Iberoamerican Exposition, while the bustling university atmosphere also gives it a special air. Bookshops and fast-food restaurants stand alongside the ancient walls of the Alcazar, some of whose battlements peek through the spaces between houses. On the other side of the street, the Hotel Alfonso XIII and the university.

SEVILLA. Gran Hôtel Alfonso XIII.

The Hotel Alfonso XIII. In the Puerta de Jerez, at the beginning of Calle San Fernando, you will find the first specific example of the secular architecture that flourished in Seville during the early part of this century. Its architect, José Espiau, developed his own series of coordinates for the building which would eventually give rise to an architectural movement of the first order: Aníbal González Regionalism—a line of architecture which constantly finds inspiration by delving into the past. The building was inaugurated by King Alfonso XIII during the 1928 April Fair, but during the Republic and the early Franco regime its name was changed to *Andalucía Palace*. Ever since its opening, this hotel is where Seville's most distinguished guests stay. The entrance hall and the central patio, as well as the ceramic tiling on the walls and the main staircase, are all fine examples of the richness and high artistic quality present in modern Sevillian ceramic-work. An elegant café and one of the cities most refined restaurants are both located in the patio's galleries. Nearby, the 17th-century **Palacio de San Telmo** is the most representative example of Seville's Baroque secular architecture. The building, now the seat of the regional government, was originally designed as a nautical school for young members of the Spanish nobility interested in subjects related to the sea. The construction process was lengthy, taking over 100 years to complete, with the participation of the leading architects of the time. It was later refurbished by the Regionalist architect Juan Talavera (who converted it into a Diocesan seminary in 1900) and

again by Guillermo Vázquez Consuegra (1992). Following the decline of the Port of Seville in the mid 19th century, Isabella II put the building up for sale. It was acquired by her brother-in-law—the son of the last king of France, Louis Philippe d'Orléans—who, along with his wife, Marie-Louise, had had to flee from the Parisian *Tuileries* following the 1948 Revolution. It thus became the residence of the Duke and Duchess of Montpensier *(left)*, actually a second court set up in Seville with aspirations to the Spanish throne. Something the Montpensiers achieved to some extent by marrying their daughter, María de las Mercedes, to King Alfonso XII, after what was said to be a brief but intense courtship •*147*. In the end, María Luisa, alone, donated most of the gardens to the city (now María Luisa Park) and, in her will, bequeathed the palace to the Church. When the Andalusian government was created, the building was acquired for the seat of the Presidency.

The president of the regional government represents all Andalusians and performs the functions assigned to him by the Statute of Autonomy. The presidency is an elected position and the government is constituted every four years by the deputies chosen in the regional elections •*118*.

The **main portal** of the Palace, facing the María Cristina Gardens •*124* is an example of the splendour of Sevillian Baroque architecture, its author being Leonardo de Figueroa. The balcony, supported by telamons depicting Indians and sea monsters, is surrounded by allegorical figures from the arts and sciences related to nautical studies. All of this is presided by the figure of San Telmo. On the inside (visible by prior arrangement), a beautiful chapel has an impressive altarpiece by Duque Cornejo, frescos by Domingo Martínez and a Zurbarán depicting Maese Rodrigo, founder of the University of Seville. Juan de Oviedo's popular *Virgen del Buen Aire*, which normally presides the altarpiece, is now being shown in one of the chapels at Seville cathedral •*69*. The rest of the palace is occupied by government offices, but the large Palm Tree Patio, the staircase and the magnificent Hall of Columns are all worth a close look. The latter is the ballroom where, during the Montpensier era, Europe's most elegant aristocrats danced, such as Austria's Empress Sissi. A commemorative plaque lists all of the members of European royalty who have been guests at San Telmo. Outside the palace, on one of the building's side facades facing Calle Palos (going back towards Calle San Fernando) you will see an interesting collection of statues depicting some of Seville's most illustrious figures, sculpted by the brilliant Antonio Susillo •*119*.

SEVILLA. Fabrica de Tabacos.

The university. This huge square building, surrounded by a moat, was built during the late 18th century. Being the largest tobacco factory in the world at the time, it left an indelible mark on the city's social atmosphere, such as the famous figure of the *cigarrera,* or cigar girl. The protruding structures on the facade's corners were living quarters for the factory's management • *127.* With thousands of employees, the factory supplied the entire European continent with tobacco and cigars, the Port of Seville being the destination for the tobacco brought back from America (doctors of the period assured patients that tobacco could cure over sixty illnesses). By the mid 20th century, it became the main centre for the University of Seville, which until then had been located in a number of different places since its creation in 1502 when it was conferred to Maese Rodrigo by the Catholic Monarchs. A bronze statue of the university's founder is located on campus (Calle Palos).

The University's main portal, in Calle San Fernando, is the work of Van der Borcht, a Dutchman, and the figure of the goddess Fama is by Cayetano de Acosta. This entranceway leads to the building's residential area, now occupied by the university rectorate. A double staircase starting from the large entrance hall joins the Clock Patio and the Main Patio, the latter with a central fountain by Acosta. The rest of the building is made up of large industrial-style bays, now divided up into classrooms for the Faculties of Philosophy, Law and History. The chapel, also by Van der Borcht, is in a separate building, located to the right of the main facade. On the inside is the tomb of the famous poet Gustavo Adolfo Bécquer. Juan de Mesa's *Cristo de la Buena Muerte* (1620) *(above)* presides over the chapel, being the patron of the Students' Brotherhood and said to be the most valuable figure of Christ in the world, along with Triana's *Cachorro*.

The end of Calle San Fernando gives way to a large open space where a number of wide avenues intersect, this being the route of passage to the southern part of the city. Here, the **Plaza de Don Juan de Austria** is bordered to the left by the **Murillo Gardens • 85**, Avenida de Menéndez y Pelayo and Seville's large Court House, a building of little architectural interest and none in the way of aesthetics. It really is not the Palace of Justice that Seville deserves, having been a real *heavyweight* in legal history and protagonist of many interesting anecdotes, such as being the first— in the times of Mayor Olavide and Gaspar Melchor de Jovellanos—to dare get rid of the conservative and useless custom of donning wigs for judging.

"... the seamen brought back the habit of chewing a brownish plant, which staind their saliva yellow and gave their beards a strong smell of licorice, vinegar, spices, and many other things, none of them pleasant..."

A. Carpentier

"... Cuántas veces el genio así duerme en el fondo del alma, y una voz, como Lázaro, espera que le diga: ¡Levántate y anda!"

G.A. Bécquer

SEVILLE, THE CITY

In the **Glorieta del Cid,** you will see a equestrian statue of Rodrigo Díaz de Vivar or *El Cid,* his well-known byname owing to the exclamation of Sevillians of the era, who shouted, *'Sidi! Sidi! Sidi!'* as he rode into Seville after having defended it from the enemies of the Poet King al-Mutamid. The statue is by Anna Hyatt, wife of multimillionaire Huntington (founder of the Hispanic Society of America), who donated it to Seville for the 1929 Iberoamerican Exposition.

And to the right, a view of the university's south facade the **Glorieta del Cid,** the **Portuguese Consulate** (whic served as that country's pavilion during th 1929 Iberoamerican Exposition), an lastly, a very large open space know as the **Prado de San Sebastián.** Her the City Council is constructing an eno mous public square, a project that ha drawn considerable attention. Th Prado was the site of two cemeterie for centuries (the San Sebastián Cem etery and the so-called Poor Folk Cemetery) and this is also the gloom site where heretics were burned *Pavilion of Portugal* the stake during the Inquisition However, Seville was somehow able to react to this dread ful past and chose to locate its famous April Fair grounc here when it began to be held in the 19th century • *44*.

The lush greenery of María Luisa Park can be seen from behind its entrance, to the left of the Glorieta del Ci But before wandering through the sinuous paths of thes beautiful gardens, take a quick look down Avenida c María Luisa, with the park on its left and lined by number of buildings from the 1929 Iberoamerican Exp sition on the right. You will first see the wonderful **C sino de la Exposición** and, next to it, the **Lope de Veg Theatre**, both examples of Regionalist architecture wi

marvellous terraces—a tempting place relax. And behind another very origin white and glass-paned building—th Montpensier Restaurant—are the pavilion of Peru, Chile, Uruguay and the Unite States. The first three are now used by schools, while the latter continues to re resent the United States in Seville. Next the consulate, at the end of Avenida c María Luisa, is a quaint little castle, know as the Queen's sewing room, which is no a **Tourist Information Centre.**

The **Queen's sewing room** is situated in the gardens of the Palacio de San Telmo. Originally built as a watchtower for the Palace bodyguards, it was later used by María de las Mercedes as a sewing and embroidery room. It was no secret to people of Seville that King Alfonso XII would sneak out of the Alcazar, Seville's Royal Palace, to court her here. It was here, then, that their intense love affair began, which culminated in a royal wedding and ended sadly with the premature death of María de las Mercedes.

Opposite the Queen's sewing room is the **Glorieta de los Marineros,** built some years ago in honour of Seville's Juan Sebastián Elcano, the first man to sail around the world. From here, there is a wonderful view of the **Paseo de las Delicias,** one of Europe's most beautiful promenades, which replaced the Alameda de

Hércules as the aristocrats' favourite place for leisure •*105*. This boulevard was built in the early 19th century over what was the Camino de la Bella Flor, which led to a mill of the same name near Tablada (downstream). To the right, the **Delicias Gardens** start (opposite María Luisa Park) with the School of Dance in the foreground, occupying the pavilion of Guatemala (covered entirely with ceramic tiling with pre-Columbian motifs) and a little further along, the pavilion of Argentina (Viceregal-style, with interesting frescos by Gustavo Bacarisas inside). At a short distance, the **Paseo de las Delicias** meets Avenida de la Palmera, with its elegant buildings and mansions (you can visit some of these later, when you explore María Luisa Park and the museums found therein).

"Dónde vas Alfonso XII dónde vas triste de tí. Voy en busca de Mercedes que ayer tarde no la ví..."

Leaving the Glorieta de los Marineros, you will enter María Luisa Park through Avenida de Rodríguez Caso. To the right, the entire park area with the Archaeological Museum and the Folk Arts and Customs Museum at the far end, behind Mount Gurugú, in the Plaza de América. In the background, the monumental Plaza de España, and to the left, the rest of the park (with the Avenida de María Luisa bordering it on the outside) with a number of beautiful small *glorietas,* or arbours.

SEVILLA.
Exposición Ibero-Americana.
Vista Parcial del Parque

The Lotus Pond is a tribute to Princess María Luisa de Borbón, the generous donor of the park. The statue is by Pérez Comendador (1924), depicting Ferdinand VII's youngest daughter, sister of Queen Isabella II, who settled in Seville in 1848 after the *Tuileries* revolutionary uprising.

The *glorieta* dedicated to Gustavo Adolfo Bécquer, by Coullaut Varela, is particularly attractive. A bust of the poet, set high on a pedestal, has two allegorical figures at its foot: Wounded Love and Love that Wounds. Next to them are three other allegorical figures: Love Longed-for, Possessed, and Lost.

María Luisa Park. The gardens of the Palacio de San Telmo •*142*, donated to Seville by the Duchess of Montpensier in 1893, was designed upon the Duke and Duchess' arrival in Seville in 1848 by the French engineer Lecolant. He carried out a clearly Romanticist design, adding terrain from an old convent to the Orange Orchard and the so-called Acclimatization Garden. The gardens acquired their present-day appearance in 1914, when French designer Nicolas Forestier undertook the task of turning it into a beautiful park, a sort of oasis in the midst of desert-hot Seville.

"In countries where there is thirst, water is the most precious and essential of the elements."

FORESTIER

It was then that the structures, including the *glorietas* found throughout the park, were built. The Lotus Pond glorieta and those dedicated to Bécquer, the Machado poet brothers and the Alvarez Quintero playwright brothers, Dante, the Islet of the Ducks... The park has been considered as a place of nostalgic yearning, an Arcadian font of inspiration, a site for perpetual tribute to the renowned, a loyal companion for pleasure and a safe refuge for freedom...

The park is a virtual museum of plant species. The most emblematic tree is the orange tree (many of them from the Montpensier orchard) while the most recent additions are the ferns donated by Austria in 1992. The bald cypress can be found in the Glorieta de Bécquer, as well as on the Islet of the Ducks and Mount Gurugú. The splendid bunya pine stands out in the *glorieta* of the Machado brothers; and the jacarandas and magnolias in the Plaza de América. In spite of Seville's heat, the peculiar microclimate created within the park allows linden trees and horse chestnuts to grow under the shade of huge hundred-year-old trees. Hackberries, blackwoods, Judas trees,

sophoras and sycamores, along with the Mudejar pavilion's bristly palmettos, the carob tree on the Islet of the Ducks, the ficus in the Glorieta de Goya or the rose garden walkway... There, colourful rose bushes bloom and multiply in abundant flower beds

in the Lion Garden, the Shell Garden and in the Rosaleda de Doña Sol (the Duchess of Santoña who, in the 1940's undertook a thorough reconditioning of the park while respecting its design), the Lotus Pond, the Frog Fountain... There are also myrtles and boxes, irises, carnations and geraniums. Pansies, magnolias, wisterias, tamarinds, aspiridias...

SEVILLA. Exposición Ibero-Americana. La Plaza de España.

Plaza de España. The entire square dedicated to Spain constitutes one of the most spectacular examples of Spanish contemporary architecture. True to the Regionalist line of thought of its creator, Aníbal González, here you will find Renaissance-style designs and Baroque towers, covered with clean brick and abundant ceramicwork. It is the materialization of the Regionalist theory, always inspired by styles of the past (*"the transformation of styles of the past has always been the source for any other style"*—Aníbal González). The Plaza was the most costly and long-lasting work built for the 1929 Ibero-american Exposition, being the true focal point of that historical event. Of spectacular dimensions, it forms a semi-circle 200 metres in diameter. The fountain in the centre was a topic of controversy because the architect refused to accept it. The plaza is surrounded

by a canal crossed by bridges richly covered in ceramics. A colourful collection of benches and ceramic-tile ornamentation forms enclosures alluding to the fifty-four Spanish provinces. The buildings are now central government bureaus and the military headquarters for southern Spain.

At the south end of the park is the **Plaza de América**, an-

other wonderful example of the 1929 Iberoamerican Exposition Regionalist style. Its most characteristic elements are the uncovered brickwork, ceramic tiles and wrought ironwork. Surrounding a series of small landscaped squares with fountains in the middle, is the **Royal Pavilion** on one side, built in flamboyant Gothic style in brick and ceramic tile, with two heralds at the entrance. To the right, a beautiful neo-Renaissance-style building, now the Archaeological Museum, with one of southern Europe's best historical collections. And opposite, the popular Mudejar Pavilion,

now Andalusia's Folk Arts and Customs Museum •*150*. The entire complex was designed by Aníbal González and, throughout the years, has been inextricably linked to the successive generations of children who have come here to play with the doves.

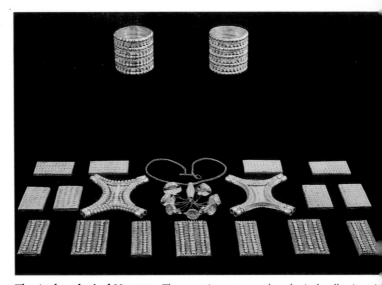

The Archaeological Museum. The most important archaeological collections in all of southern Europe are shown here, with chronologically-ordered exhibits of the numerous cultures that have settled in Andalusia. The museum's content situate it among the best of its kind, not only for its abundance of pieces but for their excellent state of conservation. The Stone, Bronze and Iron Ages are amply represented. The *Carambolo Treasure (above)* is one of the museum's most valuable collections, comprising a man's set of gold jewellery from the Tartessian civilization • *23* and • *28*. From the Visigothic era, there is an inscription by St Hermenegild and from the Roman era, the god Hermes, one of Spain's most perfect pieces of Classical sculpture.

The Folk Arts and Customs Museum reconstructs much of Andalusia's ethnological and anthropological heritage with a collection that is really worth the visit. Arranged in a circular manner, the different halls devote much of their contents to recreations of workshops depicting trades now in decline (such as a turnery, a guitar-making workshop, a potter's, a tannery, forge, wine press and cellar, etc.) Some of these collections are of considerable historical value, such as *maestro Filigrana's* castanet-making workshop or the workshop of Claudio Bernal, Seville's last barrelmaker. There are also impressive collections of Andalusian pottery and ceramic tiles, typical clothing from different periods, regional musical instruments, traditional farming tools or, by contrast, the atmosphere in different kinds of Andalusian homes (rural, middle-class, aristocratic). Another interesting aspect of the museum is its collection of original posters printed annually since the last century, announcing Seville's Spring Festivals (the April Fair and Holy Week).

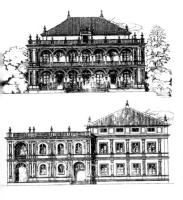

The house of Torcuato Luca de Tena

Pavilion of Cuba (1929), now a regional government office building

La Palmera. This itinerary concludes by leaving the Plaza de América and coming out onto Paseo de las Delicias once again and turning left. Here you will see the last pavilions from the 1929 Iberoamerican Exposition and the palatial architecture which flourished in Seville at the time. First, you will see the pavilion of Brazil (now the city's local police headquarters) followed by the Mexican pavilion (now unoccupied). Across the street, the pavilion of Colombia (now the Colombian Consulate). After crossing Avenida de Eritaña and the Glorieta de Méjico, you will come to the Casa Rosa • *151*. From this point on, the Paseo becomes Avenida de la Victoria, nowadays Avenida de la Palmera, a long avenue lined with huge mansions surrounded by classical gardens and which later becomes the access road to Cadiz. First, you will see the pavilion of Cuba on the right, with beautiful hardwood balconies and an impressive mirador. Further down, on the left-hand side at number 41, you will come to the Casa Sundheim, one of Seville's most interesting examples of the Modernist movement (by Hernández-Rubio, 1917). At number 46, a mirador tower, also Modernist, with medieval, pre-Columbian and English details (Fernández Balbuena, 1917). And, a little further along, at number 48, is the residence of Torcuato Luca de Tena, founder of the *ABC* daily newspaper. This particular building is one of Aníbal González' most brilliant works, with extraordinarily high-quality carved brick, wall tiling designed by the architect himself, a splendid cornice, along with impressive marble, wrought ironwork, hardwood and coffered ceilings.

The **Casa Rosa** is one of the city's few examples of Romantic architecture. Also known in Seville as *Villa Eugenia*, after the Marquise of Angulo who had it built in 1894 on the remains of the house of the previous owner (the Montpensiers' tailor), destroyed by what was said to be a mysterious fire. The entire complex has now been refurbished by the regional government and is occupied by the Andalusian Environmental Agency. Its gardens contain samples of a myriad of regional plant species and are an interesting example of Romanticist design (entrance at Avenida de Eritaña 1).

Seville is More than Seville, the Province

Bulls and Horses

The lower Guadalquivir River Basin is a mythical plain whose waters mirror two unmistakable silhouettes: that of the bull and the horse. It unites the worlds of risk and beauty under the skilful hand of the *matador*, whether it be the Sacrificial Priest of Ilipa Magna (Alcalá del Rio), the monument to the great bullfighter, Juan Belmonte, or the one dedicated to his rival, Joselito *El Gallo* in his hometown of Gelves.

Seville's geography is spotted with stock-breeding farms and pastureland for **fighting bulls.** Many of these farms allow visitors to have a look into the mysterious world of selecting and breeding fighting bulls. For example, on the road going from Lora del Río to La Campana, you can visit **Zahariche**, where the famous Miura bulls are bred.

Also interesting are the amateur bullfights and tests of bravery on young bulls offered at farms such as La Calera (in Gerena), El Triguero and El Judío (in Carmona), Camposierra (in Villaverde del Río), Arenales (in Morón de la Frontera), Juan Gómez (in Los Palacios) or El Vizir (in Espartinas).

Although closely linked to the bull, the **horse** has a world of its own, and its rituals and its popularity grow daily. There is no better way of exploring the Andalusian countryside than on the back of an Andalusian pure-bred: its slender head, penetrating look, elegant build, thick mane and tail; a friendly horse, both resistant and tame, precise in its movements, whether they be for high horsemanship, classical schooling or Andalusian *vaquero*-style riding.

This last style is traditional throughout the Andalusian countryside, where horse and rider must achieve the complicity and virtuosity needed for cattle-roping or for bullfighting on horseback, which is taught at the various **Equestrian Schools**, such as El Morrito (in Gerena), Epona (in Carmona) or at riding schools such as La Noria (in Los Palacios), the Candela Riding Club (in Almensilla) or Puerta Príncipe (in Alcalá de Guadaira), along with many others throughout the province and whose locations are listed in the appendix.

Enjoyment of horseback riding is practically unlimited, and in Andalusia you can still spend the day riding along bridle paths, cattle tracks or Roman roads without ever coming into contact with today's motorized world. Among the many possible routes on horseback, two deserve special mention.

The first starts on the Aljarafe cornice and, following paths that cross beautiful olive grove estates, passes the towns of Villamanrique and Hinojos, before entering the wetlands and the realm of the famous Rocío religious pilgrimage, and concludes on the beaches of Mazagón and Matalascañas *(below)*, the natural limits of Doñana National Park.

The second route is a climb from the town of Cantillana to El Pedroso, crossing the thickly-wooded Sierra Norte through

Constantina, Las Navas de la Concepción, Alanís, Cazalla and Guadalcanal and then descending to El Real de la Jara. This is a route of woods and thickets, fine craftwork and old anisette factories and can take between five and seven days to complete.

Each of these routes will take you through a number of extraordinarily interesting places which deserve a description of their own.

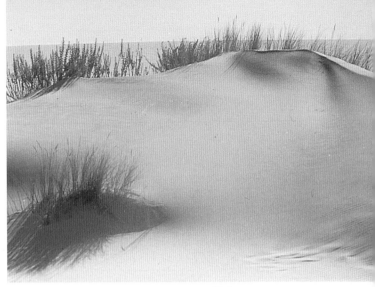

DOÑANA

Doñana National Park • _15_, declared World Heritage and a Biosphere Reserve by UNESCO, is a natural paradise situated on the right bank of the mouth of the Guadalquivir River. A stopping place for over a million migratory birds, the park is also one of the last havens for many highly endangered species such as the imperial eagle, the Iberian lynx or the white-headed duck. With over 80,000 hectares of beaches, woods, dunes and wetlands, the park contains a number of unique ecosystems which make it Europe's most important nature area. Up to 361 different bird species have been classified in Doñana, many of them wintering species from Northern Europe, while others nest or make short stopovers during their migratory journeys, attracted by its temperate climate and wetlands.

The ecosystems. Doñana's most valuable asset is the wide range of ecosystems found throughout the park. The areas near water (either river or sea) are marshland: dry during the summer, wet the rest of the year. This area has a number of peculiarities: the _caños_, or depressions; the _lucios_, or marshy lagoons; and the _vetas_, or small mounds. Parallel to the coast, there are several lagoons joining others further inland. For example, the **Santa Olalla** Lagoon, where flamingos can often be seen, together with other waterfowl such as the purple gallinule, the goose and the common duck, along with the very rare white-headed duck or the poisonous Lastase's viper... where rush, cat's-tails, reeds and cyperus thrive and the camomile and barilla plants bloom in springtime.

The so-called dry Doñana begins inland, bordered by huge shifting dunes, slowly moved by the *foreño,* the 'wind from afar'. Nearby are the famous 'bird cages' which are actually rows of centennial cork oaks inhabited by colonies of spoonbills, grey herons, night herons and squacco herons... Further inland, the lynx and Iberian mongoose roam the woodlands and rockrose scrub; the imperial eagle nests in the stone pines; flamingos and otters move about in lagoons brimming with rush and salt cedar and where deer and wild boar come to drink...

Although some prehistoric remains are still to be found in the Doñana region, its status as **Royal Hunting Grounds** since the time of Alfonso X the Wise (13th century) is much more thoroughly documented. The **Palacio de Doña Ana,** which, at the time, was property of the House of Alba, was where Francisco de Goya painted one of the most well-known portraits of the Duchess of Alba.

Goya

The property was later owned by the House of Medina Sidonia and then by the Duke of Tarifa, who built the Palacio de las Marismillas. As hunting grounds for monarchs and the nobility, Doñana was one of Alfonso XIII's favourite places, and its wildlife has remained intact throughout the present century. In 1961, the Spanish government began its assessment of the park's singular wealth while preparing its initial interventions, which would culminate in 1979 by declaring Doñana a National Park. Doñana is a world in itself, with its own inhabitants, accustomed for ages to their own particular lifestyle: making charcoal, beekeeping, collecting pine nuts and making huts and boats. People of the woods and the lagoon who can be seen skimming the water on their square, flat-keeled boats.

A VISIT TO DOÑANA NATIONAL PARK

Visits can be made in two different ways. The first is by jeep, with groups departing twice daily from the Acebuche Reception Centre (1), where there is a permanent exhibit, including audiovisuals. Since there is a 250-person limit to each tour, it is advisable to make telephone reservations in advance. In the area around Acebuche, there are places nearly perfectly resembling the park's main ecosystems, such as *La Rocina, Charco de la Boca* or *Charco del Acebrón.*

The other type of visit is by horse-drawn carriage, following the path leading from La Rocina Reception Centre to the Palacio del Acebrón, some five kilometres away.

The 'Cerrado Garrido' Nature Interpreting Station. Recently opened in the town of Aznalcázar, this marshy area includes a number of places of interest, such as the **Lucio de los Ánsares,** the **Lucio de Mari López,** the Guadiamar Biological Reserve or the so-called Marisma Gallega, or Galician Marshes. A number of protected species inhabit the area, such as the coot, goose, grey heron, flamingo, stork and purple gallinule. The reception centre is located in a huge hut, typical of Doñana, where you will find an audiovisual room, coffee shop and souvenir shop. From the same building, birds can be seen nesting in the **Lucio de las Gangas** and the **Caño Guadiamar.** Horseback-riding is also available, with 15-kilometre trails between the Station and Aznalcázar.

From around El Acebrón, you will be able to see the whitewashed walls, Moorish rooftiles and the unmistakable Baroque facade of the church honouring the marshland's patroness, Nuestra Señora del Rocío.

Sierra Norte Nature Park

Starting from Cantillana, home of the interesting craft of fringe-making for the embroidered silk shawls worn on special occasions *(mantón de Manila)*, we recommend entering the park by the El Pedroso road, crossing the Viar River, one of the three tributaries of the Guadalquivir in the park. The **Embalse de El Pintado** reservoir, suitable for both sailing and fishing (abundant pike, Iberian nose, barbel and carp), is located at the Viar River's headwaters. From El Pedroso (whose Mudejar-style church has an *Immaculate Conception* by Martínez Montañés), the gently rolling hills and the woods of holm oaks and cork oaks stretch in all their beauty right to Constantina (with a Moorish castle, Moorish quarter and the Encarnación Church with a bell tower by Hernán Ruiz), where you can see some spectacular patches of gall oaks and the very rare Turkey oak. These and other woodland ecosystems can be seen at Constantina's Forestry Museum. Further north, the triangle formed by the towns of Constantina, Las Navas de la

Concepción and Alanís contains the most rugged and hidden part of these highlands, where deer and wild boar can often be spotted in its woods and thickets. This fragrant untamed world is also a safe haven for endangered species such as the fox, the genet and the wildcat. On the northern border of the Nature Park, in the Sierra del Viento foothills, is Guadalcanal, with its three churches: La Asunción, Santa Ana and San Sebastián. From here, your route down to the district capital, Cazalla de la Sierra, will take you through

landscape of holm oaks crowned by the golden eagle's majestic flight. In Cazalla de la Sierra, the 14th-century Consolación Church, the 15th-century cloister at the Madre de Dios Convent and the excellent examples of Baroque civil architecture of the Court House, the Town Council and the Old Town Hall are all worth visiting.

In addition to Cazalla's interesting liquor and anisette factories, there is the noteworthy Hospedería de la Cartuja, in a refurbished charterhouse on the outskirts of the town, and a **Tourist Village.** Nearby, you can hear the trickling waters of the Rivera del Huéznar, or El Huéznar Brook, where there are intermittent areas with riparian forests, and where two **fishing preserves** are located. With

both a wide range and abundance of species, the small river is one of the few trout-fishing rivers in which you can still see otters on some of its more isolated bends. The entire Sierra Norte Nature Park bears the mark of the different civilizations that lived here: from the archaeological remains of the **Cuevas de Santiago** in Cazalla de la Sierra, or vestiges from the Roman era in Villanueva del Río y Minas, to the 2000 year-old traces of mining activity such as those seen at **Cerro del Hierro**, and the fascinating remains of industrial archaeology which still show, in El Pedroso, the imprint of the importance of blast furnaces and related production methods, all within the techniques and aesthetics of the mid 19th century.

The park's nearly 170,000 hectares lend themselves to all kinds of enjoyment, and specialized companies such as **Gemasol** and **Algakón** help visitors discover them all. Monitors and guides will take you down well-designed trails for the best view of the scenery and its wealth of plants and animals; you will learn first-hand about the area's rich cultural and gastronomical heritage at places like 'El Mesón del Moro' in Cazalla de la Sierra, 'La Dehesa de la Sierra Norte' in El Pedroso and the 'Mesón de la Piedra' in Constantina.

The park offers several types of visitor accommodation. Hostels in El Pedroso (La Jarosa) and Constantina, both managed by Inturjoven. And in what is called the **Reserva Verde del Huéznar**, three campsites: **Cortijo Batán de las Monjas, Dehesa del Prado** and **Fundición de la Plata**, in the **Corredor de la Plata** or Silver Corridor, formed by the old train tracks joining Villanueva and Cerro del Hierro.

In Guadalcanal, the **Cortijo La Florida,** and in Cazalla de la Sierra, in addition to the restored charterhouse and the tourist village already mentioned, there is the **Hotel Posada del Moro** and the **El Becerral** and **Las Navezuelas** cortijos. If you wish to arrange a horseback ride through the Sierra Norte Nature Park, just contact the **Al Paso** riding school, located on the road between Cazalla and San Nicolás del Puerto.

SEVILLE IS MORE THAN SEVILLE, THE PROVINCE

Horse-lovers will find many other chances for enjoying themselves. Most Andalusian towns organize competitions, but Seville's Autumn horse-racing season deserves special mention for the city's well-established **Club Pineda,** the greyhound races followed in hot pursuit on horseback by its *aficionados* and the exhibitions of high horsemanship, horse-and-carriage and cattle-roping. And you can learn about horse-breeding at the **Yeguada Militar** in Écija, or be delighted by the superb show offered by the **Real Escuela Andaluza de Arte Ecuestre** at their Recreo de las Cadenas headquarters in

Jerez de la Frontera, or at one of their frequent performances at Seville's Real Maestranza Bullring •*127*. The widespread love for the world of horses in Andalusia has also led to a profusion of fine craftsmanship, with harness makers', saddlers' and farriers' workshops open to visitors in places where equestrian traditions are most deeply rooted. However, perhaps horsemanship's greatest beauty and spontaneity can be found at Andalusia's fairs (such as the ones held in Mairena del Alcor, Seville, Ecija, Osuna, Lora del Río and Lebrija) or at the unforgettable *romerías* (pilgrimages to local shrines), a mixture of religious faith and gaiety, such as the *Virgen de la Encarnación* pilgrimage (Gerena), *Setefilla* (Lora del Río), *Consolación* (Utrera), *Valme* (Dos Hermanas), *Cuatrovitas* (Bollullos de la Mitación) or the Rocío Pilgrimage, held at Whitsuntide, and by far the most popular of all.

THE ALJARAFE

West of Seville, between the Guadalquivir and Guadiamar rivers, is an unforgettable area called the **Aljarafe** which, as its Arabic name indicates, is a slight rise in terrain which maintains one of the most fragile and subtle balances between culture and nature. Small towns with white-washed houses and Moorish roof-tiles, separated by distances easily covered on foot or horseback, combine their charm with a centuries-old unchanged landscape planted with grapevines, olive trees and orange trees. The miraculous balance between architecture and landscape, between the weight of history and the breath of life, together with its enviable climate—praised by early Arab geographers such as al-Idrisi—make the Aljarafe area a sought-after place of residence for many, where, from the time of the Romans and Moors, its villas and country houses have displayed a succession of marble, decorated wall tiling and garden ponds.

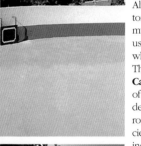

Although the Aljarafe is crossed by the A-49 (E-01) motorway which connects Seville and Huelva, we suggest a much quieter and more enjoyable approach to the area, using the traditional routes that criss-cross the region, and which are ideal for trekking, cycling or horseback riding. The first part of the route takes you from the town of **Castilleja de la Cuesta** (where you can visit the churches of Santiago el Mayor and La Concepción, and the Palacio de Hernán Cortés) down the road to Gines, flanked by roadside inns and restaurants—'Mesón Pepe Cubero', 'Hacienda San Ygnacio', 'La Taurina', and 'El Tronío'—passing olive-growing country estates such as 'Marchalomar', until reaching **Espartinas,** home of the famous bullfighter *Espartaco*, where you can visit La Asunción Church and, at 'Casa Pedro' restaurant, try the *caldereta*—a beef stew— with a glass of Pata Cabra wine. At the **Hacienda 'El Vizir',** there is *vaquero*-style horse schooling, amateur bullfights, a 700-seat covered pavilion, conference facilities, and a delicious variety of regional cuisine.

Just outside Espartinas is the Franciscan convent of **Nuestra Señora de Loreto,** with a graceful ceramic-tile cross in its atrium and an 18th-century church by Diego Antonio Díaz. **Our Lady of Loreto** is venerated at the main altarpiece, which was paid for by a bishop from Guadalajara, Mexico. Also interesting are the Mudejar-style *Aljibe*Cloister and the San Francisco Solano Chapel with a magnificent 16th-century Philippine crucifix made of ivory.

Turning south, you will be able to see the **Hacienda de Tablante** estate, which Alfonso X donated to his loyal followers and where the poet Juan de Arguijo lived in the late 16th century. Following a bridle path lined with orange and olive trees, the archiepiscopal town of **Umbrete** soon comes into view. Like most of the surrounding towns, Umbrete is famous for its *mosto*, or young wine, which can be tasted either at the wine cellars themselves or in the town's many bars and restaurants, especially between November and February. The art of seasoning olives is also practised with exceptional skill. Here, you can visit the 18th-century Consolación Church by Diego Antonio Díaz, built with brick and masonry; inside, there is a magnificent Baroque altarpiece by Pedro Duque Cornejo, presided by an image of the church's patroness, and in the transept, four 'foreign' saints, new figures of devotion brought in the early 18th century with the change of dynasty and imposed by the town's patron, Archbishop Salcedo y Azcona, who also built the Archbishop's Palace opposite the church with its elegant Neoclassical gardens.

Leaving Umbrete on the SE-627 road going south and after crossing the A-49 (E-01) motorway, another typical olive-growing estate comes into view: **Torre las Arcas**. And just a short distance away is **Bollullos de la Mitación**, whose tower at the Church of San Martín resembles that of Umbrete's.

In a pine grove on the outskirts of town is the very notable **Cuatrovitas Hermitage**, a former Almohad mosque which was later reformed for Christian worship, with its graceful detached tower adorned with horseshoe and multifoil arches. To the east, although outside the town limits, is the San Ygnacio de Torrequemada hacienda, one of the most beautiful and distinguished around Seville.

In places now within Seville's metropolitan area, there still remain fine examples of rural and stately architecture. For example, the haciendas **Santa Eufemia** *(above)* and **El Carmen,** in Tomares. However, if you go slightly north, through **Camas** and up the Zorro hillside, you will reach **Castilleja de Guzmán** with its Church of San Benito, Hacienda de La Pastora, and the former palace of the Count and Countess of Castilleja de Olivares, now a university residence hall.

In nearby **Valencina**, three extraordinarily important **Megalithic monuments**, gallery dolmens at Cueva de la Pastora, Matarrubilla and Ontiveros.

On the same road to Extremadura, some 14 km from Seville in the town of Santiponce, there are two other noteworthy points of interest: the San Isidoro del Campo Monastery and the Roman city of Italica.

SAN ISIDORO DEL CAMPO

The buttresses of the apse and the battlemented sanctuary are illustrative of the bellicose times in which the monastery was built, between the 13th and 14th centuries, by the Cistercian Order and on the wishes of Alfonso Pérez de Guzmán *El Bueno,* whose remains lie alongside his

wife's, María Alonso Coronel, in tombs sculpted by Juan Martínez Montañés, who is also the author of the old church's three-ply altarpiece, as well as a side altarpiece of the Virgin Mary with Baby Jesus, St. Joachim and St. Anne. Pay special attention to the magnificent choir stalls, the chapter house's ornamentation and the two cloisters, that of the Dead and of the Evangelists, with 17th-century frescos painted over other very interesting ones from the 15th century.

THE ROMAN CITY OF ITALICA

Founded in 206 BC by Scipio Africanus Major, this was the first Roman city outside the Italian peninsula, residence of many illustrious lineages and birthplace of two great emperors, Trajan and Hadrian. The city attained a period of splendour in the 2nd century AD and expanded considerably, adding residential areas and luxurious public buildings such as baths, theatres and a huge amphitheatre. What had up to then been a simple Roman municipality became a colony with a certain degree of independence that legislated some of its own laws.

The generosity of Hadrian, emperor at that time, resulted in the city's expansion towards the north, the part that has been excavated in recent times, while the original Italica remains beneath the municipality of **Santiponce.**

The main areas open to the public are the forum on the hill called Cerro de los Palacios, the great amphitheatre and the baths.

One of the most striking aspects of the residences excavated in Italica is their **mosaic** pavements, many still in their original locations and others preserved in the Seville Archaeological Museum.

The amphitheatre at Italica is considered to be one of the largest in the world, with a capacity of 25,000 persons. Since this was much more than required for the population, it confirms the thesis that the city was a rest and recreation centre for the legions.

Seville is More than Seville, the Province

Why Italica was abandoned remains a mystery. It is not known when this too[k] place nor the exact causes, although it is known that the bishops of Italica a[t] tended the Council of Toledo in AD 693 and Leovigild ordered the reinforcing o[f] the walls around that time. A 10th-century manuscript describes it as an abar[n] doned city stripped of its luxurious marble, and by the Middle Ages it had lost i[t] original name and was known as Old Seville.

Only the interest of scholars such as Rodrigo Caro in the 17th century, plus th[e] later efforts of a few enlightened individuals and archaeologists of the 19th an[d] 20th centuries, have made the full importance of Italica known as the first Roma[n] city outside Rome.

The **Seville Archaeological Museum** • *150* gives us an idea of the archaeolog[i] cal wealth of these ruins in its collection of superb pieces taken from the hill[.] The statue of the god Hermes, Diana the Huntress, the deified emperor Trajan in his toga, the bust of Hadrian wearing embossed armour with the head of Medusa, and the marvellous Venus of Italica carrying a lotus flower and flanked by a dolphin, are all witness to the splendour of those days and make it essential to visit both the ruins and the museum.

About twenty kilometres from Seville along the A-49 (E-01) motorway linking the city to Huelva, you come to **Sanlúcar la Mayor**, one of the best examples of how the Gothic style that came down from the north was combined with the sensitivity that came up with the African light, resulting in a vibrant Mudejar style. It is evident in the pointed arches and polygonal apse of the church of San Eustaquio in the upper part of the town; the church of San Pedro, next to the old wall, whose facade combines cusped arches, tiles and Gothic windows; and especially the Mudejar parish church of Santa María with its three naves, horseshoe arches and panelled ceiling.

Also of interest are the Chapter Granary and the local pottery, which recreates the best of the Hispano-Moresque tradition. Not far from the town is **Hacienda Benazuza**, converted into a hotel with 25 double rooms. Three restaurants, gardens and swimming pools, plus a heliport, complete this unique setting.

A few companies specialising in **equestrian tourism**, such as Equiberia, organise routes from **Sanlúcar la Mayor** through the district of El Aljarafe in groups of up to eight riders, accompanied by an experienced guide who knows the terrain, and a 4-WD support vehicle. One of the most interesting takes the visitor from **Sanlúcar la Mayor** to **Benacazón** (churches of Santa María de las Nieves and La Vera Cruz, hermitages of Castilleja de Talhara and Gelo) and from there to **Cuatrovitas**, already mentioned, and back to the starting point through **San Ignacio de Torrequemada**. Another recommended **bridle path** likewise begins in **Sanlúcar la Mayor**, crosses the Aljarafe and penetrates into the dense pinewood of **Aznalcázar** (Mudejar church of San Pablo), which borders on another world—the **routes through the Entorno de Doñana nature park**.

Seville is More than Seville, the Province

If you drive down the A-49 (E-01) motorway towards Huelva and turn north instead of south, very close to **Espartinas** you come to the charming village of **Villanueva del Ariscal.** One of its attractions is the **Góngora** winery with its impressive 16th-century screw press that provides an historical and cultural illustration of the wine-making tradition.

Somewhat farther north is **Olivares**, seat and origin of the seigneury of the same name. The holder of the title, Gaspar de Guzmán, Count and Duke of Olivares, was a powerful favourite of the king and was portrayed by Velázquez. A result of his devotion is the majestic collegiate church of Santa María de las Nieves, which houses several noteworthy paintings from Zurbarán's workshop. The same plaza is also the location of the ducal palace, and nearby is La Vera Cruz chapel.

Another recommended route starts in **Bormujos**, (church of La Encarnación, convent of Santa María la Real with a magnificent *St. John* attributed to Juan de Mesa) and follows the road to **Mairena del Aljarafe**, passing by **Hacienda La Peregrina** to the right and **Hacienda Cristo de la Mata** to the left in the direction of **Tomares**, very close to **El Zaudín**, where one can enjoy the amenities of a restaurant, horseback riding, paddle tennis and **golf club.**

The other two golf courses in the province of Seville are the **Real Club de Golf de Sevilla** (km 3.2 on the Seville-Utrera road near Montequinto) and **Golf's Country La Rocina** on the road from **Aznalcázar** to **Isla Mayor**, at km 0.8.

THE SILVER ROUTE

In Roman times, a legendary road led from **Italica** to **Emerita Augusta** (Mérida), extended on to **León** and **Astorga**, and left its mark on the western part of the peninsula through its renowned wealth and activity. Silver taken from the mines of Sierra Morena was coined for use in the cities and flowed northwards to support the military efforts of the Roman legions. The echo of that name still remains in some of the towns and the mark of mining activities in others along the south-north axis that today is part of the national road network linking Andalusia and Extremadura.

To the right of this road in the direction you are driving is **Guillena**, in whose municipal district are the ruins of the **Roman road** that was the silver route, and the settlement known as Torre de la Reina, in memory of Doña María de Molina.

Some outstanding buildings are the Neoclassical town hall with its singular facade of large pilasters, and the originally Mudejar parish church of Nuestra Señora de la Granada, dating from the end of the 14th century. The main altarpiece is Baroque from the mid 18th century. It has also a magnificent Renaissance carving of *Nuestra Señora de la Granada*, by Jerónimo Hernández, from 1578.

To the left of the road is **Gerena**, perched on a crag and marked by the culture of the granite that abounds in the surrounding area. It is one of the towns immortalised in the engravings of Höfnagel's *Civitates Orbis Terrarum*, which gives an indication of its fame and importance in the 16th century. In addition to an abundance of Roman and Moorish ruins, it also has one of the few Paleochristian churches preserved in Andalusia.

The Inmaculada Concepción parish church is a Mudejar building containing a sanctuary with three apsidal chapels, covered by octagonal vaults over pendentives, one of which supports the bell tower. The main altarpiece dates from the 18th century, and other items of interest are the 16th-century Flemish crucified Christ and the Pietà panel in the sacristy.

The main altarpiece in the church of San Benito, formerly a hospital and hospice for the poor and today the seat of the Vera Cruz brotherhood, contains an 18th-century image of *Christ of the True Cross* (the brotherhood's patron) and an attractive *Virgen de Guadalupe* from the early part of the same century. The chapel of the *Virgen de la Soledad* displays also a recumbent Christ inside an 18th-century polychrome wood-and-glass case.

The town has preserved the tradition of the local band and organises a jubilant pilgrimage festival on the last Thursday of May in honour of its patroness, the Virgin of the Incarnation.

AZNALCÓLLAR

A name linked to a long-standing mining tradition, evidenced in the numerous abandoned mines along the river **Crispinejo** and the mighty Roman and Moorish fortifications on the hill known as **Cerro de Castillo**. Through the thicket one can see the ruins of the aqueduct that supplied Italica from Tejada.

Today the town has one of the largest opencast pyrite mines in Europe.

The parish church of **Nuestra Señora de la Consolación**, with its elegant brick portal by Antonio Matías de Figueroa, is an important landmark. The chapels called La Cruz de Arriba (upper cross) and La Cruz de Abajo (lower cross) illustrate this peculiar dichotomy so common in Andalusian folk religious practices.

Towards the east, much deeper into the Sierra del Pedroso, is the village of **Castilblanco de los Arroyos**, which in times past lay along the only route between Andalusia and the plain of **Castile**, and was the setting for Cervantes' novel *Las dos doncellas*. The parish church of El Divino Salvador, originally Mudejar and remodelled in the 18th century, has a magnificent altarpiece designed by Francisco Dionisio de Rivas, made in 1655. This same artist is also attributed with the design of the altarpiece carved by Francisco de Arce in 1580, dedicated to the town's

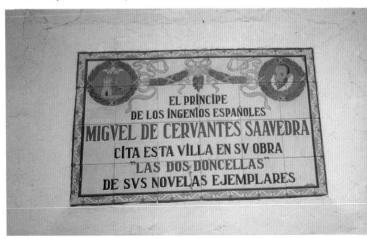

patroness, the Virgin of Grace, whose festival is held on the 4th-6th of August. The last Sunday of August is the time for a pilgrimage festival to the hermitage of San Benito, located in a beautiful mountain setting. The N-630 national road forks at **El Garrobo** (good hunting preserves and the church of La Inmaculada Concepción, dating from the 15th and 16th centuries), striking out in two directions that promise great things for the traveller. The road to **Aracena** and its sierra will take you into one of the most unusual woodlands of Andalusia, passing through **El Castillo de las Guardas** (15th- and 16th-century parish church of San Juan Bautista atop the hill overlooking the source of the Guadiamar River).

The other fork leads to Extremadura and crosses Sierra de Tentudía where you can see the village of **El Ronquillo** (church of El Divino Salvador and hermitage of Nuestra Señora de Gracia). The mayor of this town became famous during the War of Independence for killing one of Napoleon's couriers in the place still known today as Dead Man's Culvert.

To conclude this silver theme, it is well worth paying a visit to **Almadén de la Plata**, which minted its own coinage and also had copper deposits and rich marble beds that attracted the notice of the geographer Ptolemy.

The town offers good hunting of small and large game, excellent honey and mild home-made cheese, and its parish church of Santa María de Gracia has a magnificent tower by Hernán Ruiz II and Vermondo Resta. There is an image of Christ bearing the cross on its 16th-century altarpiece.

SEVILLE IS MORE THAN SEVILLE, THE PROVINCE

DOWN THE RIVER

The Guadalquivir River enters the province through Soto Cerrado, at the point of confluence with the Genil, its largest and most regular affluent, bringing crystalline water from the snows of the Penibética Mountains. And so this fine river, carrying a yearly average of some six thousand cubic hectometres, arrives at **Peñaflor**, where archaeological remains appear everywhere, reminders of its importance in Roman times. This is particularly evident in the sarcophagi, altar stones and Latin inscriptions in the atrium of the hermitage of Nuestra Señora de Villadiego.

A place to visit in **Peñaflor** is the 18th-century church of San Pedro, designed by Matías de Figueroa, with its beautiful drum dome crowning the transept.

The main altarpiece is Neoclassical, with an interesting silver eucharistic ark dated 1794 and an 18th-century carving of St. Peter *ex cathedra*. In the sacristy is a

curious polychrome jasper table and a set of wooden drawers decorated with stone chips, all dating from the 18th century.

The old Franciscan convent of San Luis is a church in the shape of a Latin cross with a single nave under a barrel vault, and the transept is topped by a beautiful semicircular dome adorned with stucco carvings. There is an interesting image of the Crown of Thorns by the Dutch painter Gerard Housthort.

The Baroque hermitage of Nuestra Señora de la Encarnación was extensively restored in the 19th century. The hermitage of Nuestra Señora de Villadiego is built against the side of an octagonal medieval tower; in addition to the modern, predominantly displayed image of the Virgin it takes its name from, it also contains a number of Roman tablets and a votive altar from the 2nd century AD.

Downstream from **Peñaflor** the river flattens out and meanders through Sotogordo and El Rincón before coming out into what is known as the Lower Guadalquivir, bordered by cane fields and rich irrigated farmland. Finally the silhouette of a large metal bridge announces the proximity of **Lora del Río**, an attractive town in the northeast of the province whose economy was given a dynamic thrust by the arrival of the railway in the present century.

Numerous archaeological sites are to be found in its municipal district, such as Setefilla, containing remains of Agar and Late Bronze Age cultures, and an Iberian necropolis. **Lora del Río** is the old Roman Axati, and remains of this culture are commonly found here, particularly relating to oil production and river traffic.

The church of Nuestra Señora de la Asunción *(left)* is Seville Mudejar, with three naves and a quadrangular main chapel. The altarpiece, originally from La Merced convent, dates from the 18th century. There is an interesting triptych in the sacramental chapel, commissioned by Ruiz Pérez de Cazalla in the mid 16th century. The church has a noteworthy collection of liturgical gold and silver works, such as the 15th-century Gothic censer and the processional monstrance, made in Seville by the craftsman Palomino in 1868.

The vault over the transept in the convent of La Inmaculada Concepción is especially beautiful. And the church of Jesús Nazareno is marked by its unique brick facade with slotted pilasters topped with vases, the work of the architect Diego Antonio Díaz in the mid 18th century, who designed several churches of this type throughout the archdiocese of Seville.

In the sierra is the hermitage of Nuestra Señora de Setefilla, with three naves, originally Mudejar and refurbished in Baroque, which houses the image of this virgin and is the scene of a popular pilgrimage festival on the 8th of September.

Lora has a beautiful Baroque town hall whose brick wreathed columns give it special character; the town's secular architecture is particularly interesting, especially the Casa de los Leones and the Casa de los Quintanilla.

Towards the north in the foothills of Sierra del Pedroso is **La Puebla de los Infantes** with its church of Nuestra Señora de la Huerta, built in the 15th and 16th centuries; the virgin to whom it is dedicated is represented in a beautiful carving dating from the early 16th century.

If you cross the metal bridge over the **Guadalquivir** you come into a fertile plain which is the extension of the valley known as La Vega de Carmona, where you will find the village of **La Campana**, historically linked to the House of Alba.

Its Neoclassical church is dedicated to Santa María la Blanca; it contains a magnificent altarpiece, designed in part by Alonso Cano, who is also the creator of the Immaculate Conception and the sanctuary door showing an image of Christ tied to a pillar. Noteworthy also are a 14th-century image of the Virgin of the Consolation and two large 17th-century paintings by Felipe de Ribas depicting St. Peter and St. Paul.

In the old San Francisco convent is an 18th-century image of the Immaculate Conception which presides over the altarpiece, polychromed to look like jasper. Also of note is the dome decorated with stuccowork that covers the church of San Lorenzo.

This entire area is particularly interesting as it is one of the places where the resettlements ordered by Charles III in the second half of the 18th century took place. The peculiar style of the New Settlements shows up clearly in many of the old houses of **La Luisiana**, its town hall and the Baroque church of La Inmaculada Concepción. The ethnographic traces of the resettlement are also still apparent in the local customs; eggs are dyed at Eastertime and the nearby village of **Cañada del Rosal** still celebrates the *baile de los locos* (dance of the mad), clearly German in origin, during the feast of the Holy Innocents.

Returning to the Guadalquivir River, you now find it wide and powerful, leaping over the dam at La Piedra de la Sal just before it receives the salt waters from the Corbones River to the left and the crystalline water from the Huesna Brook to the right. You are at the head of the irrigation zone in the lower Guadalquivir valley, one of the great farming areas of Europe.

On the right bank is **Alcolea del Río**, a site of exceptional archaeological wealth, whose pottery workshops supplied amphoras for oil and wine to the ships that plied the waters between Roman Baetica and the rest of the empire.

This abundance of archaeological sites is due to the proximity of two major Roman towns: Arva and Canama.

Nearby in La Aceña are ancient mills, and the village's church of San Juan Bautista has an elegantly decorated ogee arch in the Spanish Gothic style and a marble baptismal font dating from the 16th century. On the left bank is **Tocina**, whose La Soledad shrine stands above the town with its graceful buttresses and lantern-topped dome. The early 18th-century church of San Vicente has a beautiful 17th-century statue of St. Anne and the Virgin.

On the right bank, deeper into the sierra, is the irregular shape of **Villanueva del Río y Minas**. The cusped and horseshoe windows with alfiz denote the 14th-century origin of its Mudejar church of Santiago el Mayor. These are the most interesting details in the church, along with the late 15th-century Gothic beams and wrought-iron pulpit.

The mining operations of the 19th century gave rise to another populated area where the villas are made with pitched roofs, and whose church of San Fernando is built in the purest Regionalist style of Aníbal González.

Very close by are the ruins of the Ibero-Roman settlement of **Mulva** or **Munigua**, conscientiously excavated by the German Archaeological Institute to reveal a majestic church of Hellenistic flavour with twin access ramps. The forum, baths and other buildings led to major archaeological findings, such as a bronze tablet with the only preserved letter written by the emperor **Titus** (dated September, AD 79) and a beautiful head of *Hispania*, all of which are on display at the Seville Archaeological Museum • *150*.

There was a ford over the Guadalquivir at **Cantillana**, which left its mark on the town's history and made it an obligatory place of passage and a site of great strategic importance.

It belonged to the Order of St. James and the Archbishop of Seville for a time and was then purchased, together with Brenes and Villaverde, from King Philip II by a wealthy Corsican, Juan Antonio Vicentelo de Lecca, who became the first **Count of Cantillana** in 1581. He was responsible for restoring the parish church of Nuestra Señora de la Asunción, following plans by Diego López Bueno. Its magnificent sanctuary altarpiece came from Carmona and part of it was carved by Jerónimo Hernández in the late 16th century.

Well worth a visit are the 15th-century church of San Bartolomé, built in the style of a basilica, the hermitage of Nuestra Señora de la Soledad, and the curious craft workshops where the women, with consummate skill, put the fringes on the traditional embroidered silk shawls known as *mantones de Manila*. An interesting event is the pilgrimage festival in honour of the Divina Pastora, or Divine Shepherdess, held on the last Sunday of September.

At the threshold of the irrigation zone watered by El Viar Canal is **Villaverde del Río**; the 16th-century altarpiece inside its 18th-century church has an admirable carving of St. Anne and the Virgin.

On the opposite bank is **Brenes**; its splendid Mudejar church of La Inmaculada Concepción with three naves dates from the late 15th century and still has an elegant pointed brick portal from that period. The main altarpiece and many of its paintings are the work of Luis de Figueroa in the 17th century, while others are by Juan del Castillo.

The river makes a sharp bend around **La Rinconada** before heading towards **Alcalá del Río** dam, site of the ancient Roman town of Ilipa Magna. Its Mudejar church of La Asunción sits on Roman foundations, and the main altarpiece is the work of José de Carvajal in 1700. In an alcove is a carving of the *Assumption* attributed to Duque Cornejo and on the wall a splendid carving of *Madonna and Child with St. Anne* by Roque Balduque in 1557.

The altarpiece in the church of La Inmaculada Concepción contains elegant paintings by Hernando de Sturmio, from 1547, the same year as the creation of the Gothic reliquary dedicated to St. Gregory of Ossetia.

SEVILLE IS MORE THAN SEVILLE, THE PROVINCE

Of particular interest is a small chapel dedicated to St. Gregory of Ossetia, founded by the Catholic Monarchs in 1460; the altarpiece has an image of this saint, together with St. Gregory the Great and St. Bartholomew. There is also a 16th-century *Christ of the True Cross* and a 17th-century *Resurrected Christ,* in addition to a curious baptismal font made from a Roman stela resculpted in the time of the Visigoths. At the foot of the wall is a mural depicting St. Gregory of Ossetia and a group of donors, perhaps the king and queen themselves, dating from the early 16th century.

On the left bank of the river looking southward is **La Rinconada**, where there is a splendid square 15th-century Mudejar church with a polygonal sanctuary. On the wall is a Calvary scene with an especially dramatic expression on the face of Christ, dated 1500.

Now nearly within sight of **Seville** the Guadalquivir River comes to **La Algaba**, amid orange groves and fields of grain, cotton, corn and beets. The shining white houses are dominated by the Torre de los Guzmanes, a

square Mudejar military tower erected in 1446 by Juan de Guzmán, lord of the manor. The church of Santa María de las Nieves was originally Mudejar but underwent a major restoration after the Lisbon earthquake of 1755. The main altarpiece, dating from the mid 18th century, is dominated by the *Virgin of the Snows* surrounded by images of saints originally from a Franciscan convent.

This convent was also the origin of a magnificent image of *Christ of the True Cross,* dated 1626. The altarpiece dedicated to St. Martha has a superb sculpture of this saint dating from the late 16th century. Also worthy of visiting are the chancel to see the organ designed by Francisco de Acosta in the 18th century, and the neo-Gothic chapel by Juan Talavera next to the church.

In addition to preserving the deep roots of the bullfights and folk traditions of its September fair, La Algaba also lights candles and lanterns, or *candavelares,* on the eves of special days, particularly the feast of the Immaculate Conception.

The cornice of El Aljarafe drops into a sharp depression whose slopes are dotted with the villages along the right bank of the Guadalquivir, marked by the history and culture of the river. The entire bank is covered with flora from across the sea, brought by the galleons from the Indies that sailed up the river for so many centuries. The air bears the echo of the last riverside caulkers and carpenters, and everywhere are the signs of culinary imagination and devotion to good flamenco song, or *cante*, which tends one of its main lines—devoted to the subject of water—from Triana to the ports. **San Juan de Aznalfarache,** an impregnable Moorish fortress decisive in the defence of Seville, is the site of a church and monument to the Sacred Heart of Jesus.

Carrying on down the river you come to **Gelves**, where you can buy unusual pottery wares made at its crafts school. This is the site of **Puerto Gelves**, the first inland marina built in Spain, with a capacity for 300 boats on the water and in dry dock. It is also a residential and commercial area. Places to visit are the monument to the bullfighter Joselito *El Gallo*, near the house where he was born, and the church of Santa María de Gracia next to the old palace where the Countess of Gelves lived; she was the muse of the poet Fernando de Herrera.

Farther along is **Coria del Río**, with its church of Nuestra Señora de la Estrella and the hermitage of La Vera Cruz, where there is a treasured Roman stela dating from the 2nd century AD. River cuisine is available at Casa Márquez, featuring bleaks *a la lata*, shrimps prepared in many different ways and shad roe.

On the way to La Puebla is the house where the Father of the Andalusian Homeland, Blas Infante, made his home. It is called *Santa Alegría* and, among many other memories, preserves a study exactly as its master left it. He was married in the church of Peñaflor, in the foothills of Sierra Norte de Sevilla.

In **La Puebla del Río**, whose archaeological remains date from the Lower Palaeolithic, is the church of Nuestra Señora de la Granada with a 16th-century crucified Christ, and the hermitage of San Sebastián. On the outskirts, 22 km from Seville, in an area where bulls and horses are raised, is *El Rocío* Ranch, run by two brothers, Angel and Rafael Peralta. Both are master *rejoneadores*, bullfighters on horseback. The ranch has a capacity of more than 1500 persons in a climate-controlled setting, plus riding facilities and a bullring, and offers a full range of events centring on horses and bulls.

It features exhibitions of horses pulling carriages, mares and studs, show riding, equestrian fantasies, bull running, visits to see fighting bulls, horse schooling in the *vaquero* style, bullfighting on horseback and on foot.

Farther along you come to edge of the marsh, which is evident in the cuisine (unforgettable duck with rice at *Venta El Cruce*) and the low population density. But this will not keep you from meeting with a few pleasant surprises, such as in **Villamanrique de la Condesa**, whose church of Santa María Magdalena has an altarpiece reliably documented as made in Seville by Juan de Oviedo, Diego López and Francisco Pacheco.

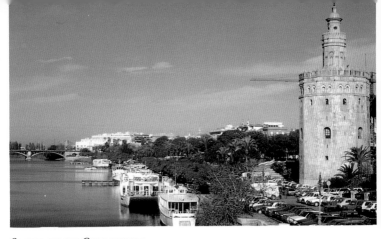

SAILING ON THE GUADALQUIVIR

There are tourist boats to take you on excursions from the wharf at the Tower of Gold in **Seville** to **Sanlúcar de Barrameda.** If you decide to make the journey in your own boat, you must be aware of the currents, which can be as much as six knots, and the lighted buoys at night.

The route goes first under the **old Alfonso XIII bridge** next to the **recreational port of Seville**, and then under the huge **Centenary bridge**, past the shipyards and through the locks where the water level changes. Then you come to **La Punta del Verde**, entrance to the protected nature area of **Brazo del Este**. Opposite **Puerto Gelves** the reeds, chestnut trees, blackcaps and bulrushes make up an ideal habitat for sultana birds, squacco herons, purple herons and other aquatic birds. Between **Coria del Río** and **La Puebla del**

Río the sailor comes across the first bleak-fishing boats and, farther along, elver and shrimp boats, with their curious nets spread wide. Now and then you can spot crayfish catchers along the bank, sleeves rolled and hard at work.

The landscape passes through gentle transitions, until you come to the Doñana marshes and finally the river's mouth at the Atlantic Ocean and the beautiful area of **Sanlúcar de Barrameda**, the town to the left and Doñana Park to the right.

LEFT BANK OF THE RIVER

Part of the never-ending adventure of discovering rural Seville is the left bank of the Guadalquivir. Stretching out from the capital city is a carefully cultivated, fertile plain rich in archaeological findings and easy of access by the Seville-Cadiz N-IV road.

If you start at the Bellavista residential area and go down the old road to **Dos Hermanas**, which crosses the Lower Guadalquivir Canal, you will come to the first singular example, the estate known as **Hacienda de Doña María**, which owes its name to María de Padilla, wife of Peter I the Cruel. It is a stunning place with its whitewashed crenellated buildings, myrtle and palm trees.

Hacienda Bujalmoro

If you use the N-IV road as an axis, the tracks leading off to the right will take you in succession to four of the most superb and accomplished examples of **rural Seville architecture.**

The first is **Hacienda de San Miguel de Montelirio** (access at km 3.8 on the SE-687 road). Farther ahead is the impressive 18th-century estate known as **Hacienda Maestre** (at km 552 on the N-IV road); its two large patios have independent entrances, one for residents and the other for labourers. It is crowned by a magnificent watchtower.

The next is **Bujalmoro** (at km 560.4 on the N-IV road), whose traditional look is enhanced with neo-Mudejar details. And the last is **Ibarburu** (at km 557.6 on the N-IV road), unmistakable and majestic with its play of red ochre and white-washed mouldings.

Hacienda Ibarburu

SEVILLE IS MORE THAN SEVILLE, THE PROVINCE

All of this springs up before the traveller in a wide open space of vibrant light, emerald green when the grain is high, golden at harvest time. The olive groves are said to produce at their best here—exceptional, select fruits for table and oil, grown fat and large under the watchful eye of the La Giralda.

You are now between **Dos Hermanas** and **Los Palacios**. The former is a very active, densely populated town where you can visit the Roman ruins of Orippo, the church of Santa María Magdalena with its interesting 18th-century altarpiece, and the Mudejar hermitage of Valme restored in the 19th century. **Los Palacios,** like the entire area, is a treasure trove of Roman ruins and was the home of Andrés Bernáldez, priest of Los Palacios, chronicler of the Catholic Monarchs. Its church of Santa María la Blanca has a 17th-century altarpiece painted by Pablo Legot, and in the chapel of Nuestra Señora de los Remedios is a 17th-century Archangel Michael by Pedro Roldán.

Down the road a bit more you reach **Lebrija**, the ancient Nebrissa of the Romans, who considered it a seaport and endowed it with a splendid dock beside the lake formed by the Guadalquivir at that time. *"Here is where Father Bacchus laid the foundations for the walls,"* says **Elio Antonio de Nebrija**, author of the first Spanish Grammar. The people of Lebrija are proud to be the children of Bacchus rather than Hercules; they know about wine, sing like nobody else and organise a 'May Crosses' festival that amazes the visitor.

Elio Antonio de Nebrija

The town's main church, **Santa María de la Oliva,** is perhaps the most interesting in Andalusia; it starts as a 13th-century Alphonsine church and ends up with an altarpiece where the chisel of Alonso Cano and the brushes of **Pablo Legot** joined together to produce an image of the Virgin of the Olives that has all the vigour of the fully ripe fruit

whose protectress she is. On the wall of the church is a memorial to **Juan Díaz de Solís**, citizen of Lebrija who reached the Río de la Plata in Argentina.

The church of Santa María de Jesús has a 16th-century image of Christ of the Good Death; in Barrionuevo, where the May Crosses bloom and the people sing and dance around them, there is a magnificent crucified Christ of the True Cross in the chapel of the same name.

THE GREEN TRAIL

At the southern edge of the province is a little-known route which runs from **Arcos de la Frontera** to **Olvera** and **Almargen**, following a railway line that was planned under the dictatorship of Primo de Rivera and abandoned with the outbreak of the Civil War. The Green Trail traverses a magnificent landscape of rocky terrain and thick brush and today can be explored on foot, on horseback or by bicycle.

The **Guadalete River** valley stretches from Arcos to Olvera, and further ahead is the **Guadalporcún River**, whose stunning rapids race through the narrow gorges of **Peñón de Zaframagón** before coming into view of the undulating outline of the town of **Olvera.** All along the Green Trail are a variety of ecosystems, such as behind the Arcos reservoir, wooded areas with patches of ash and poplar trees, thick scrub and meadows of holm oaks, wild olives and carob trees. The Peñón de Zaframagón is a nesting place for a colony of griffon vultures, the largest in Andalusia, while hawks, tawny owls, Bonelli's eagles and common vultures abound in the rocky places along the river.

The weed-choked tunnels of the old railway are an exciting challenge to fans of adventure tourism, while the residual infrastructure of the line—abandoned stations, halts, service huts, etc.—is ideal for recreational, educational and tourist purposes as facilities for cultural and other types of activities.

Especially noteworthy among the lodging places in this area is the new *El Peñón* tourist complex at Algámitas, located in an extraordinarily beautiful rugged setting, with restaurant and campground, and mountain refuges soon to be built.

Historic Towns
in the Countryside

If you want to get closer little by little to the other reality of Seville, that of the towns scattered round her countryside, perhaps a good place to start is the C-432 road from Seville to Utrera. Along it you will find the estates of **El Rico, La Andrada** and **Santa María,** near the crossing with the road from Dos Hermanas to Alcalá de Guadaira, and farther along the estates of **La Concepción** and **Mateo Pablo**, which enrich the vernacular rural architecture with Baroque and urban elements from the late 18th century.

Soon you come to **Utrera**, its houses overlooked by the blind, whitewashed towers of the old mills, and the peculiar colours of its golden ochre arches and dark-green doors throughout the town. The chronicles tell us that it was here, in Utrera, where the Count of Vistahermosa set the standard for the image, aesthetics and breed of the fighting bull. The old castle was razed by the Catholic Monarchs and restored by the Town Council when democracy was instituted, and today is the site of terraced gardens, a restaurant with memorable *tapas*—those famous snacks served with drinks—and an **auditorium.**

Two defiant towers, **Santiago** and **Santa María,** are visible from the terrace. The former has exquisite Gothic carvings beneath its basket-handle arch and an image of the Magdalene attributed to Duque Cornejo in its altarpiece, in addition to a black Christ of the Order of St. James, a talisman against epidemics.

The second tower rises next to the church. Its first section was beautifully executed by **Martín de Gaínza**, and the second, more austere, by **Hernán Ruiz.** There are still two more sections, which elevate the Baroque rhetoric of the bell gable to the highest heavens.

In the **Hospital de la Resurrección** are two recumbent sepulchral images of knights of the House of Arcos, **Lope** and **Juan Ponce de León.**

The Franciscan church, formerly Jesuit, has a vault with painted frescoes depicting the *Triumph of the Society*, attributed to **Juan de Espinal**, and the church of Las Hermanas de la Cruz has an image of the *Virgin and Child* by Jerónimo Hernández. The old **Palacio de Vistahermosa** later became the property of a philanthropic *indiano* (name given the emigrants to Latin America who later returned to Spain) who also financed a **theatre**, subsequently restored.

Serafín Álvarez Quintero

Joaquín Álvarez Quintero

Today the palace is the town hall and next to it is the house where the playwrights **Serafín** and **Joaquín Álvarez Quintero** were born.

Very close to the town is the shrine of La Consolación, built with a single nave in the early 17th century, where the Virgin of the Consolation is worshipped; her image *(left)* dates from the 15th century. She is the patroness of the city and the district, and since the end of the 18th century the festival celebrated in her honour each year brings together for ten days thirty brotherhoods and over twenty thousand people. With a bit of luck, you can hear good flamenco song at Peña Curro de Utrera, opposite Santa María, and for very little money taste the local sweets, *mostachones*, Franciscan treats served and eaten on the rough piece of paper they were baked on.

Alcalá de Guadaira

The town's coat of arms bears a castle and two keys, which could symbolise bread and water, both supplied to Seville from Alcalá. The water came from its prodigious underground springs and flowed through the aqueduct that terminates at the gates of Seville, while the bread was made in centuries-old bakeries. A **Roman bridge** with six arches stretches across the **Guadaira River** and the town stands beneath the silhouettes of the eleven remaining towers of its Almohad castle, scene of fierce fighting in the 15th-century rivalries between the **Ponces** and the **Guzmans** and the Peninsular War in the 19th century. Another tower appears above the castle from the Mudejar **hermitage of La Virgen del Águila**, dating from the 14th century as certified on the facade under the nave. Other interesting sights to see in the town are the Baroque altarpiece in the **church of Santiago** and the 14th-century Mudejar **church of San Sebastián.** Near the town is the **Oromana Park**, one of the most popular, luxuriant and enjoyable in the province, home to the pleasant three-star Hotel Oromana *(below)*.

The countryside around **Alcalá de Guadaira** is unrivalled, with its foliage, water and old mill. Its beauty captivated numerous painters, such as **Arpa, Alperiz, Bacarisas and Hohenleiter**, not to mention the great but accursed painter who lived next to the *Adufe*, **Romero Ressendi**, nor the master engraver and artist **Paco Cortijo**.

Between **Alcalá de Guadaira** and **Mairena** the landscape settles down into low rolling hills that are an inexhaustible trove of archaeological wealth, from **El Viso** to **Carmona**. It was all lovingly investigated by **Jorge Bonsor**, so that today we have the opportunity to see a major part of these archaeological findings on display at the **Bonsor Museum** in **Mairena.**

The area also contains some of the best **rural architecture** in superb examples of **olive-growing country estates** such as **La Caridad, Hacienda Guzmán, La Soledad, San Antonio de Clavinque, Los Miradores, Hacienda Santa Ana** (Mairena del Alcor) and **Palma Gallarda.** The last one mentioned has unusual wall tiling and a graceful bell gable.

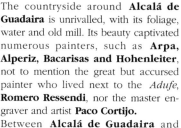

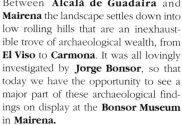

SEVILLE IS MORE THAN SEVILLE, THE PROVINCE

CARMONA

The **Puerta de Sevilla** *(above)* opens westward; it is built with Punic ashlars and an Almohad horseshoe arch, and marks the entrance to the ancient Roman town of Carmo, whose houses march up the hill to the **Puerta de Marchena** in the *Alcázar de Arriba (below)*. Today the inner bailey of this 'upper alcazar' is the site of a **Parador de Turismo**, a hotel run by the state. Along the way are the churches of **San Blas**, surrounded by a whitewashed labyrinth reminiscent of the old Jewish quarter; **San Bartolomé**, with a remarkable 17th-century image of the Nazarene by **Francisco de Ocampo** and other major Late Gothic paintings; and **El Salvador**, a Jesuit church with a noteworthy altarpiece by a local artist, **José Maestre**.

A bit further along is the Plaza de San Fernando, site of the town hall and a favourite place for Sunday strolls beneath its palm trees and traditional street lamps. To one side is the old town hall and a singular 16th-century Mudejar building, and opposite is a series of elegant facades dating from the 17th century.

Surrounded by emblazoned palaces belonging to the families of **Aguilar, Rueda** and the **Marquis of Las Torres** is the priory church of **Santa María**, enclosed within a patio of orange trees, heritage of the mosque that it was, sculpted in the Gothic style from base to transept. Its remarkable vault is the work of **Diego de Riaño.**

In addition to the image of the patroness of Carmona, the 14th-century **Virgin of Grace,** there is an Immaculate Conception by **Duque Cornejo** in the sacramental chapel and a magnificent altarpiece bearing the signatures of **Nufro Ortega and Juan Bautista Vázquez** from the 16th century.

e chapel dedicated to St.
seph has an altarpiece by
artín de Gaínza and pan-
s by **Pedro de Campaña**.
rther up you come to the
rium of **Santa Clara** con-
nt with its watchtower
vered by a four-sided
ping roof; inside the
urch is a 17th-century al-
rpiece by **Felipe de**
bas. This building is on
e same corner as the
ospital de la Caridad,
th its interesting 16th-
ntury patio; and on the
est of the hill looking to-
ards the **Puerta de**
órdoba is the **church of**
antiago. Its facade is
udejar and the tower is
orned with *sebka*, or
rved brickwork, while
e three polygonal apses
nd belligerent, in a men-
ing gesture toward the
ntier with the infidel.

rmona has good places to stay, such as the **Parador** *(above)* which re-creates the
mptuous atmosphere of the alcazar of King Peter, and the **Hotel Casa Palacio Casa**
Carmona *(right)* with 30 rooms, combining the formal elements of the 16th
ntury with elegant decoration and the
st advanced catering technology.

e **town festivals** are celebrated in hon-
r of St. Matthew with a pilgrimage festi-
l on the 21st of September; other impor-
nt dates are the feast of the Virgin of Grace
the first Sunday in September, the May
ir, Carnival in February and Holy Week.
ere is an impressive **necropolis** on the
tskirts of the town.

ÉCIJA

The town is famous for its many towers, light and haughty with their smooth bric
walls, nearly all built or reconstructed after the Lisbon earthquake in the 18th centur
which caused extensive damage throughout the area. The parish church of **Santa Cru**
was likewise affected and restored by **Antonio Matías de Figueroa**; it preserves a
image of the Virgin of the Valley by **Jerónimo Hernández**, and its altar is an imposir
Paleo-Christian sarcophagus from the 5th century showing the Good Shepherd amor
biblical scenes in the aesthetic tradition reminiscent of the old Roman city, capital of th
Conventus Astigitanus, one of the four Roman judicial districts of ancient Baetica. Rc
man traces are also to be found in the elegant mosaics preserved in the town hall.

Écija is a city of numerous convents, including **Santa Florentina** with an excellent altarpiece from the workshop of **Pedro Roldán**; **La Concepción**, or the Moroccan convent, with a beautiful Mudejar coffered ceiling and memorable confectionery recipes; and **Las Teresas**, with interesting Mudejar interlacing arches. The church of **Santiago** is noted for its altarpiece with 16th-century panels by **Alejo Fernández**, a crucified Christ by **Pedro Roldán** and another altarpiece from the workshop of **Pedro de Campaña**. The church of **Santa Bárbara** has a magnificent set of Rococo choir stalls and fantastic shapes in its Mudejar coffered ceiling. The 18th-century church of **Santa María**, with square floor plan, has a tower strongly reminiscent of Seville's Giralda. Also of note are the beautiful 18th-century towers dedicated to St. John and St. Anne.

The secular architecture is also remarkable, particularly the **palace of the Marquis of Peñaflor** *(left)* with its majestic double staircase that arises directly from the horse block, and beautiful balcony spanning the entire facade.

Another exemplary building is the handsome Valdehermoso Palace, located just opposite the former, noted for its 16th-century plateresque facade.

The cuisine of Écija features such delicacies as 'Moroccan cakes' and *yemas*. A good time to visit the city is Holy Week, the Spring Fair early in May or the Autumn Fair at the end of September.

SEVILLE IS MORE THAN SEVILLE, THE PROVINCE

ARAHAL

This town sits atop a gently sloping hill next to the road linking Seville and Malaga. Its name is Arabic and its past linked to fighting, as it belonged to the Military Order of Alcántara until **Pedro Girón** purchased it in 1461 to make it part of the land belonging to the House of Osuna.

The brotherhood of **La Caridad y Misericordia**, formerly part of the old Hospital de la Misericordia, walks in procession during Holy Week, according to its rules of 1501. There were also Franciscan, Minim and Dominican convents.

Today the Franciscan convent is **San Roque**, and the remaining Dominican convent is **El Rosario** with its elegant atrium. The church of **La Magdalena** stands in the shadow of the Duke of Osuna's patronage, sustained until the

middle of the last century. The feast of its patron saint, the Magdalene, is celebrated on the 22nd of July, and the festival of *El Verdeo* is held in September, in joyous celebration of the coming of the grey clouds that bring gentle rain, and with the rain, work and wages for the winter.

Leaving Arahal in the direction of Seville's Sierra Sur, you come to **Morón de la Frontera**, which in its day was a major border outpost. The town's lords fortified it with their various Roman, Moorish and Christian walls, parts of which are still standing in a high part of the town known as *El Gallo*, today a lookout point.

Near the town is to be found a beautiful old farmhouse called *Cortijo de Arenales* where you can enjoy horseback riding, *tientas* or fights with young bulls, gaming and many other activities.

Morón has magnificent churches (San Francisco, Nuestra Señora de la Victoria, San Ignacio and others), and some of the outstanding features of its secular architecture are its palaces, such as the one belonging to the Marquis of Pilares with its stately gardens

MARCHENA

This town is enclosed amid battlements and towers. The square Islamic ones are made of adobe, while other later towers from the time of the wars between the feudal lords are round and made of stone.

Marchena was the birthplace and seat of the seigneury that gave the town its name, in the person of **Rodrigo Ponce de León**, lord of Marchena and the first Duke of Arcos, the best captain from Castile in the conquest of Granada, who succeeded in taking **Loja**. Here he attended mass, seated behind lattices on a platform in the church of **Santa María de la Mota** *(left)*, a jewel of the carpenter's art with its whitewashed pillars and dark coffered ceiling. The Baroque altar is presided over by St. Mary herself. In a chapel alongside is a recumbent Christ by **Jerónimo Hernández**.

Next to **Santa María** is La Inmaculada convent, in whose atrium the once-and-again whitewashed wall is broken by an ancient revolving window through which the nuns sell their delicious quince preserves.

Over the main altar in the church of **San Juan** is a splendid Gothic altarpiece with fourteen panels painted by **Alejo Fernández**, and a strikingly beautiful alabaster sculpture of the head of St. John the Baptist on a platter by **Pompeyo Leoni** or **Juan Bautista Vázquez**. In a chapel to the left is another Gothic altarpiece and a handsome wood carving of *St. Ignatius Loyola* by **Martínez Montañés,** the head made of lead. An adjoining building contains the Museum of Religious Art where one can admire nine of Zurbarán's canvases, a large processional monstrance made by Francisco de Alfaro en 1575 and a remarkable collection of silver and gold items, books and old habits.

In the heart of the town is an historic crossroad formed by the old road from Carmona to Osuna—from the crown territory to the lord's dominions—and the old road from Écija to Morón—from the frying pan to the forge. The crossing is known as *los cuatro cantillos* (the four stones) and is a miniature agora, a gossip corner, a distillery of the best flamenco song, an obligatory meeting-place for conspirators and would-be town criers. Amid the well-preserved murals is the Puerta de Sevilla, also called Arch of the Rose, which leads to the street of the same name and the old quarter of the town.

In **Marchena** is a chapel called **La Vera Cruz** containing a **Pietà** by Juan Bautista de Amiens, and a group of green crosses on the white wall, an anchor and a pathetic Gothic Christ.

Opposite *los cuatro cantillos* was the Dominican quarter, a convent founded by the duke in 1517 whose altarpiece has a magnificent *Christ of St. Peter,* near the ducal mausoleum. Going up Calle de las Torres you come to **San Andrés**, which houses a 16th-century *Pietà* by **Morales, *the Divine***, and the old **Santa Isabel** Jesuit convent, with a noteworthy Renaissance painting by **Roelas** and an Immaculate Conception by **Alonso Cano.**

The unusual decoration in the 18th-century church of **San Agustín** shows Indian-looking angels peering out from behind vegetation that is decidedly American.

The traveller can't leave Marchena without paying a visit to the extraordinary **Lorenzo Coullaut Valera Museum**.

If you arrive in **Marchena** during Holy Week, you can witness the curious ceremony of *el mandato* (the mandate), hear the typical Marchena *saeta* sung, and taste the spinach prepared specially for these feast days.

There is a local fair held so that its final day coincides with the last Sunday of August or the first Sunday in September. Its *casetas,* lanterns and attractions follow the traditional Seville model.

OSUNA

The old town is unforgettably beautiful; the long winding streets bordered by iron gratings all meet in the **Plaza Mayor**, with its fountain and town hall facade that curves gracefully as if it may have had too much sun. Behind the windows of the old casino lurk drowsiness and a row of wicker chairs. The visitor enters the plaza between **San Carlos el Real** and **La Concepción** convent, whose nuns make quince preserves and ring-shaped cakes known as *roscos de San Blas*, among other delicacies. The whole town is a carefully orchestrated, hierarchically organised place where the ducal seal is embedded in the landscape to become part of the geography, culminating in the **collegiate church** with its plateresque Puerta del Sol, a distant relation of the one in the Lily Room in the *Signoria* of Florence. It is the golden maturity of the Renaissance style which triumphs here, an air of Italy that returns with the dukes; the first, **Pedro**, was Viceroy of Naples, as were the third and fourth dukes of Osuna, while the fifth came to be governor of Milan.

Such is the atmosphere inside the collegiate church, where you can admire a marvellous **Calvary** scene by *El Españoleto*, a crucified Christ by **Juan de Mesa** and the chapel of **El Santo Sepulcro,** burial place for the lineage. The entrance is through a tiny square patio which combines the best of the Andalusian plateresque style, in exquisite stuccowork, with the gracefulness of its segmental arches. Half the history of Spain lies buried in the church's **pantheon**, from **Juan**, father of the

founder and patron of Christopher Columbus, to **Catalina**, granddaughter of Hernán Cortés and wife of the **Grandee Osuna**, lauded in **Quevedo's** verses.

There are also three important altarpieces in the collegiate church: at the main altar, reconstructed in the 18th century; in the chapel of El Sagrario, dating from the 16th century; and the Virgin of the Kings, also from the 16th century. The church contains some of José de Ribera's major paintings from the 17th century, such as *The Expiration, Martyrdom of St. Bartholomew, St. Jerome, Tears of St. Peter* and *Martyrdom of St. Sebastian.* There is also a major collection of gold and silver religious items and a few singularly interesting parts of coffered ceilings.

But in addition to an exceptional pantheon and a remarkable collegiate church, what most characterises the founder **Juan**, fourth Count of Ureña, as a patron was his decision to create a **university** in his own, which he himself financed. He laid down its regulations, drew the plans, endowed the chairs and provided grant funds—all in 1548. He funded the construction of the prominent square building which changed the life of the town and

its district, creating a source of knowledge and a way of life that left its mark on graduates and rectors, on famous doctors of medicine an theologians, in the habit of studying, comparing and drawing conclusions. The 16th-century oratory is perhaps the most beautiful in Osuna.

Returning to the old part of the town, you will observe that its extraordinary architectural wealth centres on two places.

Opposite the **Palacio de Puente Hermoso**, one can visit the Carmelite convent of **San Pedro**, with its 15th-century Mudejar facade and several noteworthy altarpieces. Across the street is the church of **El Carmen**, containing a magnificent Renaissance altarpiece by **Juan de Oviedo**, and a striking set of choir stalls. Nearby, in the **Espíritu Santo** convent, is another extraordinary Baroque altarpiece with St. Augustine, St. Blas and the Immaculate Conception.

The second point of interest, especially for secular architecture, is the **Chapter Granary**, built in the 18th century according to drawings by **Ruiz Florindo**, with the highly ornate decoration, flowing line of the eaves and wrought iron that give the facade force and personality. Close by are the 16th-century **palace of the Marquis of La Gomera** and the **old Audiencia**. Not far away is the church of La

Victoria, where the Nazarene comes out to procession on the night of Good Friday, and the church of **Santo Domingo**, with its extraordinary altarpiece by **Diego de Velasco** and **Jerónimo Hernández** dating from the late 15th century.

Not everything can be the severity of stone, and you can buy 'dog biscuits' at **La Encarnación** and admire the 18th-century tiling on its cloister walls. Delectable 'brown cakes' and *caspiroletas* are on sale at **Santa Catalina**.

If the traveller doesn't favour sweets and wants a change of scene, he or she can find good wine and perhaps hear truly authentic flamenco song amid the yellowed photos and bulls' heads of old taverns like El Jondón, El Café Nuevo and La Reforma. Going along La Carrera just before returning to the Plaza Mayor, to the right is an ancient hat shop which is a hallmark of the past and makes a very interesting photo.

Up the hill leading to the **collegiate church**, set in the Torre del Agua, a 14th-century water tower, is the **Archaeological Museum • _150_**, which displays reproductions of Iberian reliefs preserved in the National Archaeological Museum in Madrid and the Louvre in Paris, along with very interesting pieces from the Iberian, Roman and Visigoth civilisations, all found in Osuna, which makes this museum even more singular.

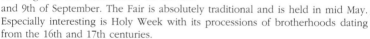

Osuna celebrates its town festival on the 12th of January, the feast of **San Arcadio**, and also organises a pilgrimage festival for the Virgin of the Consolation on the 8th and 9th of September. The Fair is absolutely traditional and is held in mid May. Especially interesting is Holy Week with its processions of brotherhoods dating from the 16th and 17th centuries.

Hunting on horseback with dogs is one of the town's most characteristic sporting activities and attracts a large number of enthusiasts.

Estepa

Driving east along the A-92 highway, the landscape from **Osuna** onward becomes more rugged. To the right are the mountainous areas of Cerro de las Ánimas, Cerro del Martillo and Sierra Becerrero and round a bend in the road **Estepa** comes into view, perched on a hill overlooking the valley of the Yeguas River which joins the Genil on the border of the province. At the top is the church of **Santa María**, which evidences several styles from base to tower, ranging from the 15th to the 19th centuries. **Estepa** was sold to **Adán Centurión** in 1599; one of his descendants, **Juan Bautista**, ordered the building of two convents which still mark the horizon: the Franciscans and the Clares.

In the church of **Los Remedios** are a striking altarpiece, work of the Ecijan master **Cerreño**, and reliefs with gospel themes in the alcove. One of the interesting sights in the town is the **Victoria tower**, built in 1790, svelte of line, with five sections and sculpted spire. Another place worth visiting is the church of **El Carmen**, whose luxuriant polychrome Baroque facade, sculpted with select marble, is one of the first examples of that exuberant Baroque style that is so widespread in the south of the province of Cordova.

There is a very interesting Baroque facade on the **palace of the Marquis of Cerverales**, and a visit to the factory that makes *mantecados*, the sweet that assured the town's prosperity, should not be missed.

On leaving **Estepa**, after passing **La Roda de Andalucía**, you come to the salt-water **Fuente de Piedra Lagoon**, covering 1400 hectares. This is one of the few breeding places for flamingoes, along with the French Camargue and Coto de Doñana.

Sierra Sur

Between Morón and Estepa is a gentle curve in the mountains that marks the southern edge of the province. Known as the Sierra Sur, it rises little by little and becomes sharper, shaping a complex mountainous landscape from the sierras of El Coronil and Montellano to the Osuna and Estepa ranges. It is close to the so-called **Moorish band** and shares its complexity of character and wealth of cultural syncretisms, the fruit of centuries of frontier life.

Following the Mudejar uprisings in the late 13th century, the entire area was pacified by fire and iron, castilianised and occupied by military orders: Calatrava in Osuna, St. James in Estepa and Alcántara in Morón. They gave the urban landscape and collective life a fighting mystique and a military aesthetic.

SEVILLE IS MORE THAN SEVILLE, THE PROVINCE

Algámitas is at the foot of Peñón del Terril. Its name is of Hebrew origin—*halgami* meaning rock—and it is located in a beautiful setting, although it has no buildings of particular historical importance. There is a municipal campground set in an enchanting landscape known as *El Peñón*.

Coripe is traversed by the 'Green Road of Sierra Sur', which passes through the most stunning, rugged landscapes on the entire route, dotted with viaducts and tunnels along its incomparable way. The town is located at the confluence of two rivers, the Guadalporcún and the Guadalete, and its old part surrounds the church of San Pedro, restored in the last century. The 'burning of Judas' is celebrated on Easter Sunday.

Los Corrales is where the Roman ruins of Ilipula Minor are to be found. Its 18th-century parish church is dedicated to St. James the Elder.

Martín de la Jara, named after its founder, Captain Martín de Angulo, has a curious salt-water lake, called Laguna del Gosque, that is home to a variety of water birds. There is a noteworthy 16th-century crucified Christ in the church of Nuestra Señora del Rosario.

Montellano, with its white houses, is set between the Guadalete and Salado rivers. It has interesting Bronze Age archaeological sites, the Gothic Cote Castle—an example of 14th-century military construction along the frontier—and the 18th-century church of San José.

Pruna owes its name to the stands of plum trees that abound in the hills surrounding the town. Its 16th-century parish church was built under the patronage of the Ponce de León family.

La Puebla de Cazalla lies along the edge of the Marchena countryside and the left bank of the Corbones River. Its castigated Moorish roots are the source of the town's excellent flamenco singers, or *cantaores*: La Niña de la Puebla, Diego Clavel, José Menese and Manuel Gerena.

The 16th-century parish church of Nuestra Señora de las Virtudes houses an excellent collection of Andalusian Baroque images, and there are still significant ruins of the old Moorish castle standing by the river.

El Saucejo sits alongside the Corbones River in the foothills of the Penibética mountain range. In its parish church of San Martín is an unusual pulpit made of red jasper.

Villanueva de San Juan has an 18th century parish church, San Juan.

El Coronil is thought to have been the old Celtiberian and Roman town of Salpensa. It has an old Roman bridge over the Guadalete and a spectacular 14th-century frontier castle, Las Aguzaderas. Other places to visit are the church of Los Remedios and the old La Trinidad convent.

Los Molares castle, although surrounded by the old town, is still imposing with its crenellated walls that were so decisive in the wars with Granada. Built in 1336 by Lope Gutiérrez de Toledo, parts of it and a few gates are still in good condition.

The parish church of Santa Marta is Mudejar in origin and was remodelled in the 18th century. It houses a good sculpture of St. Clare dating from the mid 17th century.

The poet Baltasar del Alcázar, author of *Cena Jocosa*, lived in the castle as its alcayde. The festivities celebrated in July in honour of the town's patroness, St. Martha, were known as the 'kerchief festival' because of the importance of the silk trade in the town.

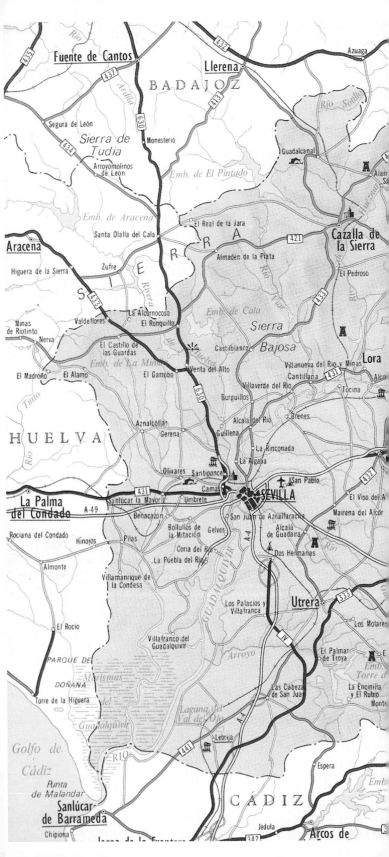

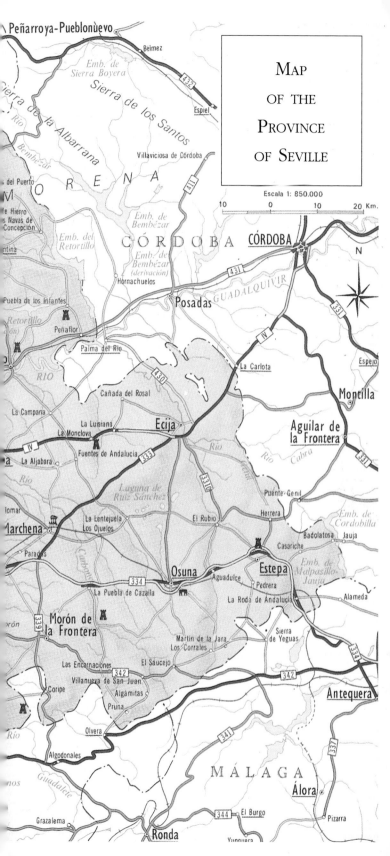

MAP OF THE PROVINCE OF SEVILLE

Escala 1: 850.000

10   0   10   20 Km.

General Index of Place-Names, the Province

GENERAL INDEX OF PLACE-NAMES, THE CITY

**PATRONATO PROVINCIAL
DE TURISMO DE SEVILLA**

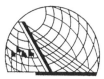

SEVILLA CONGRESS AND
CONVENTION BUREAU

Andalucía

RIO DE